Presidential

LEADERSHIP

Presidential LEADERSHIP

FROM WOODROW WILSON TO HARRY S. TRUMAN

Robert H. Ferrell

UNIVERSITY OF MISSOURI PRESS   COLUMBIA AND LONDON

Copyright © 2006 by
The Curators of the University of Missouri
University of Missouri Press, Columbia, Missouri 65201
Printed and bound in the United States of America
5 4 3 2 1   10 09 08 07 06

Library of Congress Cataloging-in-Publication Data

Ferrell, Robert H.
    Presidential leadership : from Woodrow Wilson to Harry S.
Truman / Robert H. Ferrell.
        p. cm.
    Summary: "Examines the personal styles of presidents Woodrow
Wilson, Warren Harding, Calvin Coolidge, and Harry Truman.
Uses the diaries of Colonel Edward House and White House
physician Joel Boone and other sources to examine presidential
decision making. Incorporates comments on Hoover and Franklin
Delano Roosevelt. Includes interview with historian John
Garraty"—Provided by publisher.
    Includes bibliographical references and index.
    ISBN-13: 978-0-8262-1623-6 (alk. paper)
    ISBN-10: 0-8262-1623-4 (alk. paper)
    1. Presidents—United States—History—20th century.
2. Political leadership—United States—History—20th century.
3. United States—Politics and government—1913–1921.
4. United States—Politics and government—1919–1933.
5. United States—Politics and government—1933–1953.
I. Title.
    E176.1.F475   2005
    973.091'09'9—dc22   2005023511

☯ ™ This paper meets the requirements of the
American National Standard for Permanence of Paper
for Printed Library Materials, Z39.48, 1984.

Designer: Kristie Lee
Typesetter: Phoenix Type, Inc.
Printer and binder: Thomson-Shore, Inc.
Typefaces: Adobe Garamond

Contents

Preface

IN THE chapters that follow I have sought to set out the presidents of the United States as they were, not as they appeared, and each time found myself in disagreement with my fellow historians. In that sense my judgments may well seem arguments. But I think not; rather they are restatements, new measurements made after the passage of many years and, one must say, the advantage of much new historical material. The truth is that we know far more now, can calculate far better, after the dust has settled.

And so here are judgments of Woodrow Wilson as commander in chief during World War I, 1917–1918, when he showed that he could not handle the requirements of a nation at war. His successor, Warren G. Harding, has been described as one of the nation's worst presidents, and I believe there was a virtual conspiracy of enemies and circumstances, and plain bad judgment, to make his reputation appear that way. Calvin Coolidge, now a shadowy occupant of the presidency, has been placed in the category of unsuccessful holders of the nation's highest office; he does not occupy the subbasement, where his predecessor so unfairly has been lodged, but his reputation is far below where it ought to be—so I think.

Years ago the historian John A. Garraty, an old friend, came out to Bloomington, Indiana, and he and I taped a long conversation about American foreign policy from 1919 until 1945, which here follows my judgments of Wilson, Harding, and Coolidge. The period we discuss was when, historically speaking, the great errors of the last century, the dismal twentieth century of World Wars I and II and the cold war, were made. He and I much enjoyed ourselves during that long morning of taping, and we settled many of our country's problems in retrospect. I offer the conversation here because it does seem to capture the huge problems after World War I and the failure of the American government and people, and of American presidents, to help resolve them before, in the late 1930s, everything cascaded toward war, the immense tragedy of World War II. Americans, it now is clear, had their chance to change the world. That they did not do so was perhaps, in the main, a failure of leadership. The overarching reason for the failure that did take place may have been the inability of the human mind, individually or collectively, to divine the danger of inaction, simple though that may sound.

The last of the presidents who appear in this book has become a virtual symbol of popular affection—Harry S. Truman of Independence, Missouri. I share that feeling. My fellow historians, most of them, do not. I am unsure why they insist on seeing Mr. Truman otherwise. Apart from his policies, almost all of which were enormous successes, he was such an attractive personality. If I may close with an anecdote, let me recall that in the antediluvian year 1957 a small group of scholars met at the University of Kansas in Lawrence. One morning our leader, the late George L. Anderson, related that next day we would drive over to the other side of Kansas City and meet the then former president in the newly constructed Truman Library in Independence. Half of our group groaned, for they were hardly the former president's admirers. Next morning we all went over. The president walked in, wearing his double-breasted suit, the handkerchief in the pocket folded carefully to at least five tufts. We formed around him like a group of grade-school scholars. He grinned, looked over his glasses, and asked, "Are there any isolationists in here?" Not a word from the critics. He went around and shook hands. He was such a direct, and simple, man. He came up to me, put out his hand, and said, "Truman." (What other president of the United States would have described himself that way?) I put out my hand and replied, in one of the minor anticlimaxes of the last century, "Ferrell."

Acknowledgments

Every book requires assistance, and I must thank the editors of books and journals in which the chapters originally appeared. Two anonymous readers were very helpful. And then there is the wonderful director of the University of Missouri Press, Beverly Jarrett, who allowed me to put the essays together in what I do hope is a book that makes its points. I also thank the press's managing editor, Jane Lago, for her commonsense approach to all manuscripts, which is something we academics need.

Presidential

LEADERSHIP

One

WHO ARE THESE PEOPLE?

E VER SINCE the presidency of Richard M. Nixon, scholars have been in a quandary over how much they know about presidents. Nixon, we now have to say, was unstable in personality. The signs appeared well before the discovery of the tapes, the latter an almost horrifying example of what the presidency could come to. Nor was the presidency of William J. Clinton reassuring for those of us who voted twice for him and found ourselves deceived. We begin to think that public figures, more than private ones, are intensely difficult to know. *Why* we want to know what moves them personally is of course self-evident, for the private sides of such figures, the cores of their being, often govern what they do publicly.

In my own studies of American presidents, which have resulted in books on the presidents from Woodrow Wilson through Harry S. Truman, I have had both successes and failures in attempting to estimate their personalities. My estimate of Wilson is, quite frankly, based on my experiences with academic people, of which group Wilson was one. He was preeminently an academic, theory tending to dominate experience. His first book, which made his academic career and took him from Bryn Mawr and Connecticut Wesleyan back to the Princeton he had loved as an undergraduate, was truly an academic production. It was *Congressional Government* (1885), his dissertation at Johns Hopkins about how, ever since the presidency of Abraham Lincoln, the trinity of Montesquieu, the three-part organization of government under the Constitution, had been dominated by Congress.

1

He proclaimed the fact, and it is of interest that when the academic became the politician and rose to the presidency in two years, he had this notion in mind and determined that he would not be, like his predecessors, under the yoke of Congress. This was an academic conclusion. He wrote the book in Baltimore and never went down to Washington to take a look.

One could contend that Wilson's dominance of Congress at the beginning of his tenure as president and then his gradual loss of control, until the debacle with the Senate over the Treaty of Versailles, was an academic approach. This theory of what lay at the core of his being seems to work. One might add that his belief that in the beginning was the word, that oratory could take his fellow citizens to the heights, from which they might look down and see the small, simple world, accords with his academic proclivities. Words were deeds; they could arrange actions.

To understand the presidency, we attempt our notions, our arching points, and I claim without hesitation that Wilson was an academic.

More reliable in the search for the springs of action, and what historians hope to find and perhaps in most cases cannot, is some outside, observing individual's thoughts. In the instance of Wilson, the closest one can come is the diary of Colonel Edward M. House, who considered himself a sort of amateur psychologist and wrote carefully about the man he sought to serve. House, however, was eventually baffled by his subject and took refuge in the belief that Wilson had been charmed and then dominated by his second wife, the widow of a Washington jeweler, Edith Bolling Galt, whom the president married after the death of his wife of many years, the former Ellen Axson. House is no sure guide to Wilson, for he took that president's measure for only a few years and then skewed his judgment with his dislike, verging upon hatred, for Edith Wilson.[1]

In seeking to define the personalities of presidents, it is, if necessary, acceptable to draw one's own conclusions, but it is better to measure with a yardstick offered by someone who knew his subject personally. In the case of Wilson, there is not much alternative to a writer's judgment.

In the instances of the next two presidents, and possibly the next three, a White House insider's judgment is fortunately available. The source of judgment is the memoir of the assistant White House physician, Joel T. Boone, who saw much of the Republican presidents of the 1920s and brought it all together in a massive memoir, a thousand pages on each of the chief executives. The Boone papers were opened at the Library of

Congress in 1995, twenty years after Boone's death. Few writers on the presidency have used the memoir. Indeed, to my knowledge, only one writer has other than myself: the author of a massive biography of Florence Harding that is, well, one of the worst books I have ever read, a combination of surmise and invention and psychologizing that is best left to coffee-table-book readers, that is, to be looked at but not read. Boone had been the physician for the presidential yacht *Mayflower* and was a friendly man and soon found himself almost a member of three presidential families. Years later, after retirement from the navy as a vice admiral, he enlarged on the line-a-day diary of the 1920s. The memoir is no literary masterpiece and veers from points of high interest to a litany of social events, but it is an inside view of the presidencies he knew so well. Best of all, it does not tell a scholar what these presidents thought but makes observations of what happened, and a reader can use his or her own judgment.[2]

In the instance of Warren G. Harding, Boone shows clearly that this Ohio president was nothing like the caricatures of Mark Sullivan and Frederick Lewis Allen and, notably, the newspaperman of Kansas who hated Harding with a passion because an Ohio newspaperman had become president in 1921 instead of a Kansas newspaperman. William Allen White was a highly political man and described Harding in *Masks in a Pageant* (1928) with such exaggeration, yet quotable description, as to be ludicrous. Dr. Boone saw a quiet, hardworking, abstemious president. The scenes described by Sullivan, Allen, White, and Alice Roosevelt Longworth of a bottle-filled White House replete with poker-playing politicos never appeared to the physician so frequently called to the scene.[3]

Recently going through the papers on President Calvin Coolidge, I reread an embarrassing scene—embarrassing for whom I am not sure—about his wife, Grace, who having purchased a riding habit, that of an equestrienne, asked her husband to see it as she tried it on. Coolidge came into the bedroom, looked at his beautiful wife clad in the new and modish outfit, and lost control of himself, shouting at her (screaming, said Boone, who saw what was going on), told her never to wear it again, and stalked out. What are we to make of that? Was this not a president whose nerves were stretched taut, who was self-contained to outside observers, Silent Cal to newspapermen who believed this description fitted all, but who was highly emotional, capable of poor judgments behind the mask of New

England, not at all the professional politician who scrutinized everything and made the cold, dry decisions the nation's business deserved?

Boone's drawing of the president after Coolidge, Herbert Hoover, seems less surefooted. He wrote of games of medicine ball early in the mornings, an unusual form of exercise for paunchy, middle-aged cabinet officers and other officials, the president playing ferociously in the name of exercise, willing to push a huge inflated ball into their faces, but that experience displayed few personal points. The president was not impelled to show what made him tick, Boone felt, and much of the advice the physician gave concerned one of the Hoover sons who came down with tuberculosis, a difficult malady to control during that time. Then the Great Depression overwhelmed the president, with his private physician—Boone was boosted to the rank of the president's physician, not an assistant, during the Hoover administration, with a navy captain's commission—largely looking on helplessly as the president without success sought to enlist private initiatives to defeat the awful economic turndown while, rumbling in the background, the Far Eastern crisis betokened rising militarism in Japan.

To espy any principal motive power behind Hoover still seems difficult, and his heavily written and fact-laden memoirs are no more informative than those of his predecessor, Coolidge.[4]

The presidency is such a personally driven instrument of government, and the way of individuals is so important, that any explanations of what might go up to Capitol Hill or leapfrog the Capitol to the Supreme Court to the east will haunt a researcher not at all satisfied with ordinary description. One then comes to the sphinx himself, as cartoonists drew Franklin D. Roosevelt. Suffice it to say that after half a century and more, any information akin to Dr. Boone's memoirs, or to go back to Wilson the tightly fitting academic nature of the president, might well, indeed almost have had to, come out; none has appeared, and I predict none will appear.

For all of Roosevelt's talents as a political insider, he was capable of making the greatest mistake, in politics, of any politician ever to have entered the White House in the past event-filled century, or for that matter what little we know of the twenty-first. This was the effort to "pack" the Supreme Court in 1937, which lost him the support of Congress in the years that followed. How he could have presented his preposterous notion of packing the Court, naturally denying that he was attempting to do it, boggles the mind. He should have, perhaps must have, known that this was a disastrous thing to attempt. One thinks of the later cliché—the Court was an icon of politics. It was one thing to appoint worthy politicians to the Court, whatever little they knew of the law, and the elevation of the former mayor of Detroit, Frank Murphy, was a conspicuous case in point. The same held for the attorney general who arranged the legal quibble for the destroyers-for-bases agreement of 1940, Robert H. Jackson, who needed an award for ingenuity and could lend little scholarly distinction to his new duties. Jackson made an open attack on his Alabama colleague, Hugo Black, in 1946, at a time when Jackson might well have been boosted to the chief justiceship.[5] FDR could play the game of politics with the best of its players on such issues and then made the egregious effort to enlarge the Court. Failing that, he undertook the "purge" of senatorial anti-Court-packing enemies the next year and lost that one in every contest he entered.

What made the president so skillful and unskillful is the stuff of guess-work, for none of his intimates, even Harry Hopkins, knew why. Hopkins worked incessantly for "the boss" and for a while lived in the White House and sat with, seeking to amuse, the president every evening, yet in the end he learned little about him. During Roosevelt's last year, when the president was dying of heart failure and learned what he was up against, he did not tell Hopkins, let alone his wife or children. On the extremely important issue of Roosevelt's successor, embodied in the choice of a vice presidential running mate in 1944, when it was plain to see for people close to him that Roosevelt would be reelected to a fourth term and could not possibly survive it, Hopkins was on the outside of the conspiracy by the political bosses and treasurer and secretary and, most important, national chairman of the party—an anti–Henry A. Wallace conspiracy that ended with the choice, by a slim margin, of Senator Truman.[6]

For all the books on what Roosevelt thought, what formed his ideas and actions, we have no real knowledge of what lay behind the sphinx. The late historian David M. Potter said all this years ago in a prescient article, and his judgment has held. As presidential historians, we must agree with Potter that our science, if we would so have it, is still in the area of art.[7]

We can, however, rejoice in the single president of the past century who revealed everything about himself, to wit, Truman. And this, to be sure, was through his wonderful writings. As something of a student of Truman, the present writer had heard for years, prior to an epiphany in December 1978, that Truman's private papers amounted to little or nothing, even though the president refused them to researchers after he opened his general files. His principal assistant with the memoirs, a professor of law at the University of Kansas, Francis Heller, told me that was the case, that they were full of old FBI reports, that is, cotton, hair, and rags. The memoirs, published in 1955–1956, two huge volumes, said little of the man. Heller used to bring in to the president draft chapters of the memoirs, and Truman would take them home to read, scrawling corrections in his easily identified bold hand. With the exception of several dozen pages in the first volume obviously written by the president himself, concerning early years and experiences politically prior to the presidency, the memoirs are coolly factual. Then came the opening of the private papers in the Truman Library in Independence, and never had such plain speaking (to use the title of the journalist Merle Miller's altogether unreliable book) been seen before. The private papers contained scraps of paper, hundreds of them, dated and often bearing the legend "From the Desk of Harry S. Truman" or simply "The White House," on which the president wrote what amounted to a diary. There were thousands upon thousands of letters. The historian Monte M. Poen put together the unsent letters, some of them marked "not sent H.S.T." His book displays the president's penchant for starting a letter on an even keel and then taking it overboard, relating to the addressee his several major sins and some minor ones, and what a treacherous fool he (the addressee) was.[8]

The frankness of the nation's thirty-third president has been an enormous relief to students of the presidency accustomed to the byzantine thoughts of Truman's immediate predecessor and, until the opening of the Boone papers, the inscrutability of the three (or at least two of the three) Republican presidents of the 1920s.

The president of 1945–1953 had a great sense of history (as he understood it) and liked to turn it on the political scientists and historians who were attempting to measure him and his administration. They were spreading prejudices, he would say. They were purveyors of Republican principles or else, just as bad, liberals enamored by his predecessor (whom he respected but did not love). In the nineteenth century, their wisdom was naught but a bundle of New England notions that sought to ignore the Middle West and West and confine the Union to a corner of what it became. These people did not understand statesmen like Thomas Jefferson and Andrew Jackson and Wilson—the last offered a vision of the Parliament of Man, and the unbelievers rejected it (Truman for years carried a copy of "Locks-ley Hall" in his billfold, copied over many times). The nation's thirty-third president when a youth read four volumes of biographies, which his mother bought from an itinerant salesman, ranging from Nebuchadnezzar to Sarah Bernhardt. When a rising politician, Truman read Claude Bowers on Jefferson and Marquis James on Jackson. The scholars were out to get all Democratic presidents, including himself. It was his task to set them straight. For political scientists and historians seeking the foundational ideas of their presidential figures, Truman was ideal. He possessed no sides.

Approaches to judging the presidency have varied over the years, and the usual approach, one must say, is to codify a president's actions rather than concern oneself with what might have caused them. But given the inscrutability of many of the presidents, there may not be much else to do. In some cases, such as Wilson, the nature of the man's longtime asso-ciation, life on a campus, defines him, explains why he did some things and not others, making him almost predictable. One of the senatorial "irreconcilables," who were against the Treaty of Versailles in any form, said after the treaty's defeat that he always trusted Wilson, knew what he would do, and the president did not disappoint him by compromising with wavering senators. The Wilson definition works. Dr. Boone, close to the scenes of action for Harding and Coolidge and fairly so for Hoover, is a source for those presidencies. Roosevelt is inscrutable. Truman, thank-fully, told us what he was about and why.

Two

WOODROW WILSON

A Misfit in Office

P RESIDENT Woodrow Wilson may have looked like a commander in chief, and because of the Constitution's description of the president of the United States he often found himself so described, but in truth the role was utterly foreign to his being. This chief executive has gone down in history as one of the great holders of his high office; yet his behavior during America's participation in World War I was almost never that of commander in chief.[1] The reasons Wilson did not fulfill this part of his constitutional role are many and relate partly to the time in which he lived, partly to his work as an educator—first as a professor at Bryn Mawr, Connecticut Wesleyan, and Princeton, then as president of the last institution—and partly to a personal outlook that brought him to a dislike of, almost an aversion for, military affairs and military men.

Wilson grew up in the high noon of the Victorian era when war seemed virtually abolished save for expeditions in Africa or Asia. To take part in a war between white men, between Anglo-Saxons as the usage had it, would be race suicide—to use another description of the time. Words were what advanced humankind: the words of literature, the words of oratory. Wilson

grew to manhood during this wonderful time, a poised moment in the
history of the world, and neither he nor his contemporaries had any idea
of the reckoning that was about to take place. They believed in Western
Civilization because what they saw emboldened them. All was right with
the world. For Wilson, this outlook was reinforced by his experiences in
academe, where he was quickly a huge success: the most popular professor on the campus at Princeton and afterward the first nonclergyman to
be president of that university. If the very fact of peace, he might have
thought, could not remake the world of his time, it would be possible to
educate the new generation to better ways. He lived at a time when people
took the Latin root of the word *education* seriously. "Princeton in the
Nation's Service" was the title of one of his best-known orations. A century ago Wilson and others believed in such words about education. Last,
there was the view of life that came out of this president's Scottish and
English inheritance, perhaps also out of Presbyterianism. Wilson wanted
to believe that wars were a thing of the past—that war was against the
nature of educated, modern peoples. For him even to consider himself a
commander in chief was a kind of archaism from the eighteenth century.
He was a student of English constitutional history as much as American,
and in the English tradition the navy was important and the army was
something to watch, for it could co-opt the state. European governments
had fallen victim to the danger but not the English—except during the
Cromwellian period, which was an interregnum in English history—and
the American experience paralleled the English. George Washington had
announced, although in the words of Alexander Hamilton, that the European experience was un-American. The only really large war in American
history up to Wilson's time had been the Civil War. As a native Virginian
he justified it and said on more than one occasion (which incidentally en-
deared him when election time came) that the South had "absolutely
nothing to apologize for."[2] But he did not believe that war was part of the
nation's practical experience; he did not equate the War for Southern Independence with the kind of war the Europeans were talking about.[3]

It is a curious, almost forgotten, fact that Wilson in 1917–1918 was a
complete misfit as commander in chief, so far as the nation's war economy
and the mobilization of the war department to conduct a fighting war on
the western front in France were concerned. In regard to these vital ele-
ments of war making, his behavior was paradoxical, strangely apart from

his fighting words but apart also from his reputation, which was greatly deserved, for being a leader of Congress and the nation. The president in 1917 was only a few years from his extraordinary triumphs at the beginning of his first term, when he had confounded the nation, and certainly the nation's informed electorate, by showing that he could come from governing a diminutive college and a small state, New Jersey, to lead the country, that he would not merely propose—as had countless chief executives before him—great measures for passage by Congress but would force Congress to do his will. Years earlier he had published *Congressional Government.* Upon taking office he displayed himself as no academic, no closet intellectual, but as a man who could enforce his will upon what had always been (and would, of course, be again) the most recalcitrant governing body in history. But in 1917–1918 his leadership diminished virtually to nothing, save for a sudden and for him providential reassertion of authority in the spring of 1918 that got him out of what was surely the most dangerous crisis of his presidency before the failure of the League of Nations in the Senate some months later. The student of politics wonders what possessed the president to let things go, in regard to economic mobilization for war, and, in regard to the war department, to let everything cascade into crisis.

In its top administration, economic mobilization was so badly handled that for a full year it was a travesty of what presidential administration should be. The president seemed to believe that all he needed to do was make a public statement, form a committee, and forget the problem. A later generation would describe much of what happened as a public relations problem, yet that is unfair to the president; Wilson appears to have believed that motion equaled achievement. The first formal organization to oversee what would become the war economy actually was not Wilson's doing but that of the U.S. Navy, perhaps because that part of what was then a two-part armed forces was better acquainted with industry than was the army, where manpower dominated rather than machines. The navy then had a far larger budget than the army, and most of it went for ships and maintenance, with only a small amount for men. The navy in 1916 organized a consulting board of scientists that included such prominent figures as Thomas A. Edison and Henry Ford. Its secretary, Grosvenor B. Clarkson, sent out inventory forms to discover the country's industrial resources. Thirty thousand forms came back, but the board and the secretary of the navy unfortunately did nothing with them. The assistant secretary of the navy, young Franklin Roosevelt, privately sneered at the effort, considered that industrialists knew nothing of war, and told an assistant that Ford was so ignorant of naval matters he thought a submarine was something to eat.

In August 1916, Congress—again, not the president, whose business it might have been—created the Council of National Defense, another group of prominent citizens who worked without pay and whose private concerns limited their time spent on council duties. With war getting ominously close, the council met for the first time in December and, like its predecessor, appointed a director. After the United States went to war on April 6, 1917, each member of the CND formed a committee to supervise a part of industrial mobilization. The committees produced committees, and soon there were 150. Throughout 1917 the CND accomplished little. It had three successive heads. At last the crisis in economic and military mobilization drove the president to appoint Bernard M. Baruch, a member of the War Industries Board (one of the CND's parts) as chairman of that board, to which the president gave control of the entire work of industrial mobilization. Baruch's appointment came in March 1918, and America's participation in the war was to end in November.[4]

But it is in the details of economic mobilization in World War I rather than in administrative confusion that one sees the proof of maladministration. Here it is instructive to turn to two major efforts at mobilization: shipbuilding and manufacture of powder. It would be possible to look to other programs, such as rifles, machine guns, artillery, tanks, and planes, in which there were successes with rifles and machine guns, failure with the others. The efforts to produce ships and powder, however, best illustrate how Wilsonian administration affected economic mobilization.

Undoubtedly some of the failure to turn out ships lay in the nation's near total unpreparedness for the task, for at the outset of the war it possessed a minuscule merchant marine, a very small number of ways in which to construct ships, and few workers and managers skilled in shipbuilding. The merchant marine had declined precipitously from the time of the Civil War, when attacks by Confederate raiders had driven much of the American merchant marine to foreign flags. The decline was visible indeed by 1917, when the total American oceangoing tonnage was a bare one million tons, which was about what German submarines sank in the single month of April 1917. The number of American ways had declined to sixty, for both steel and wooden ships, grossly inadequate considering the need in 1917. Ship construction had become a seldom practiced if not lost art.

More distressing than the long tradition of marine neglect were the officials whom the president installed to supervise the work of regeneration. None had experience in shipbuilding. Two had industrial experience, and the president neatly balanced them with two who did not. He first placed the Shipping Board in the hands of a city reformer, William E. Denman, who during a brief moment in the spring of 1917 enjoyed national prominence.[5] It is true that Wilson balanced the inexperienced Denman with Major General George W. Goethals, whom Theodore Roosevelt had picked out of the army's engineer corps and told to go down to Panama and make the dirt fly. In building the Panama Canal, Goethals supervised one of the world's greatest engineering feats and might have done the same with shipping in 1917–1918. Instead, he got into a public argument with Denman, who had little respect for the aging general, and Goethals submitted his resignation to the president in the summer of 1917. Wilson accepted with alacrity, asking for and receiving Denman's resignation, as if the two were on the same plane of incompetence.[6]

The president then chose as head of the Shipping Board Edward N. Hurley, who had some experience as a businessman. To take charge of the board's operating agency, the Emergency Fleet Corporation, he chose another prominent figure, the steelmaker Charles M. Schwab—but not before he had tried a rear admiral, Washington Lee Capps, as Goethals's replacement; Schwab took over in April 1918. Presumably Hurley would deal with the president, Congress, and the public, while Schwab handled the work of shipbuilding. A former assistant to Andrew Carnegie, who founded the Bethlehem Steel Corporation, Schwab moved across the country in a private railroad car urging shipyard workers to get on with their assignments. But he did not have enough time to produce the results he and the nation desired before the war ended.

With regard to ships one must conclude that almost everything that could have gone wrong did. The nation had allowed the merchant marine virtually to collapse and had nothing on which to build. Personalities chosen for the task were inadequate; lack of talent canceled out talent. Planning may have been on too large a scale. Planners decided to increase twentyfold the ways around the country, from sixty to twelve hundred.

Time did not permit such construction. The Shipping Board had to make do with confiscating ships under construction, appropriating enemy and neutral ships in harbor, and such legerdemain as bisecting lake ships to get them through the Welland Canal. The board planned to produce 2 million gross tonnage in the war's first year. It produced 664,000 tons in 1917 and 1,301,000 in 1918, far too small a tonnage considering the need.[7]

In examining the war economy it is also instructive to consider the production of powder for the American Expeditionary Forces, gathering in France under the leadership of General John J. Pershing, and see how presidential prejudice, really presidential populism, led to a second disaster for the war economy. If the war had lasted into 1919, powder production, like shipbuilding, might have sufficed. Had Pershing received the enormous reinforcements he requested—he sought one hundred divisions, each of forty thousand men, including twelve thousand support troops—there would have been great need for powder, and the final plan for its production would have supplied it. Instead a contention arose with the country's principal powder maker, the Du Pont Company, and the administration delayed for nearly a year in setting in motion an arrangement that would have guaranteed Pershing the ammunition he required. Fortunately the Allies, mainly the British, supplied it.

The story of powder in World War I is not well known; yet it stands revealed in an authorized biography of Pierre S. Du Pont.[8] The authors show that the Wilson administration's problem with the company was that Pierre Du Pont's efficiency as a powder maker and his business acumen were too much for President Wilson and Secretary of War Newton D. Baker. The Allies in 1914 had gone to the Du Pont Company with huge orders, as it was far more economical to have Du Pont produce powder than to ship to Britain or France the four to nine pounds of raw materials required to make one pound of powder. The Du Pont Company took the orders, and knowing that the resultant plants would have little use in peacetime charged the Allies enough to amortize the plants. Unlike competitors, Winchester and Remington, which financed capital expansion by borrowing against payments they would receive, Du Pont wrote off everything by charging for it. Certainly the company made a profit, and even with a retroactive tax of 12.5 percent on profits in 1916, shareholders received $62 million that year, the face value of the company's common stock.

The Du Pont Company's success, and profits, though not from American orders, excited the president and his secretary, and when the United States became involved in the war these two executives of the nation's mobilization virtually ignored Du Pont. Baruch, who in March 1917 had an advisory role in one of the Council of National Defense's committees, wrote Pierre Du Pont and inquired about the status of all raw materials needed for explosives, but that was all. Confused, the company head wrote Baker that the company's production had been taken up until September 15, 1917, inferring that if the U.S. government wanted powder it would have to arrange new plants. Baker did not take the hint. One might contend that the secretary and his superior did not know at that time whether America's contribution to the war would be largely ships and supplies other than powder or perhaps only financing of Allied war orders. Baker and Wilson may have been confused. But Wilson had sponsored a draft bill within days of the declaration, which became law in May, and a sequel would be to equip the levies so raised. It would have been wise to keep in touch with the nation's powder maker.

In the autumn, word came from the president's personal representative in London and Paris, Colonel House, that a crisis in the war was at hand. Collapse of the Russian front and the imminent dissolution of the provisional regime in Russia might allow the Central Powers to transfer hundreds of thousands of troops to the western front and bring a breakthrough in the spring. When word came from House, the war department got into action, without getting in touch with the machinery of mobilization—the War Industries Board and, behind it, Secretary Baker and the president. Major General William Crozier signed Du Pont to a $250 million contract, the largest government contract ever arranged up to that time, that included $90 million for powder plants. Within days Baker canceled the contract.

It became clear that Wilson and Baker feared giving such a contract to Du Pont, feared the public reaction. At one juncture Baker said privately that he had "just come from the White House" and the country was going to win the war without Du Pont. President Wilson appointed a western mining executive, Daniel C. Jackling, to head the powder program, and Jackling went to Du Pont and asked for help. A large contract went to a construction firm with no experience in powder making, the Thompson-Starrett Company, which insisted that Du Pont take half of it. By this time Baker realized his error, saw the possibility of losing the war without Du Pont, and allowed the Delaware company to take half, and more, of the contract. Du Pont's plant, Old Hickory near Nashville, was in production just as the war ended. On the war's last day the Thompson-Starrett plant, Nitro at Charleston, West Virginia, began production.

2

Some years before World War I, in the 1890s, Professor Wilson of Princeton taught a course on the theory of administration at Johns Hopkins University in Baltimore and took meals in the same boardinghouse as one of his young students, Newton Baker. This chance encounter was to have fateful results for the management of the war department in 1917–1918. The student went to Cleveland, where he assisted the reform mayor, Tom L. Johnson, was himself elected mayor, and made a considerable reputation championing a three-cent ice cream cone, a three-cent streetcar fare, and a three-cent admission to a municipal dance hall where young men and women could meet under wholesome circumstances. Under his administration the city made an annual contribution of ten thousand dollars to the municipal orchestra, an unheard of profligacy. Wilson watched Baker's rise with pride and in 1913 offered him a position as secretary of the interior, which the mayor declined. In 1916, with no experience with the military, Baker accepted the secretaryship of war, succeeding Lindley M. Garrison of New Jersey, who resigned after the president refused to reform the highly politicized National Guard.

Baker made a reputation in Washington. Boyish in appearance, so short in stature that he was accustomed to sitting behind his massive desk in the war department with one leg curled under him, he was almost inconspicuous standing next to the bulky generals. He was an attractive civilian figure in a forest of uniforms. On his desk was a fresh flower. His ideas were those of a reformer; he was a friend of Frederic C. Howe, with whom he had roomed in college. He made impressive speeches. He spoke so rapidly, 225 words a minute, that stenographers had difficulty following him.[9]

Baker's modus operandi in the war department pleased his military subordinates. He seemed to hold a reverence for military men, liking all the officers he met. He liked the two chiefs of staff in the critical year of 1917, Major Generals Hugh L. Scott and Tasker H. Bliss. Whatever these chiefs desired, he backed them, once saying to Scott: "You know all about this, I know nothing. You must treat me as a father would his son."[10] He informed his first biographer, Frederick Palmer, that he had learned subordination of civilians to the military from his father, who had told him of an episode involving General Robert E. Lee and President Jefferson Davis. According to the story, when Davis was giving Lee military advice the latter unbuckled his sword and handed it to Davis, who ceased the advice. Such an arrangement, Baker believed, was far more beneficial to the Confederacy than the way in which President Abraham Lincoln, Secretary of War Edwin M. Stanton, and Major General Henry W. Halleck interfered in the operations of General Ulysses S. Grant.[11] Baker thus was much like his chief, the president. His private secretary, Ralph Hayes, believed the reason Baker and Wilson got along so well, apart from their fond relationship as student and teacher, was that "their mental processes were either so much alike or so harmonious."[12] Baker looked and talked like the civilian he was. At the same time he let the war department do what it wanted.

Why Baker acted this way is not difficult to understand. He must have allowed Scott and the others to do what they wished because of a sense of his own inadequacies in military matters. He did not believe, as Elting E. Morison has shown so perspicaciously, that it was his task as a public servant to run the enterprises he presided over. Morison has written that Baker acted as if he held "a sort of pastoral office." His duty was to exhort, to elucidate, and above all to persuade, not to order or command.[13]

It is possible that Baker learned such a procedure from Wilson's course on the theory of administration at Hopkins. But one can only add that such a procedure in a brassy place like the war department in Washington was fantastically wrong. A recent biographer of Baker has written that the secretary was the head, not the figurehead, of a great and successful enterprise.[14] The first of these judgments seems difficult to believe. As for the latter, the enterprise was great, but Baker's contribution was great only in its ineptitude. Success came after Baker passed the duties of army chief of staff to Major General Peyton C. March in March 1918. This efficient general gave little attention to his nominal chief, who had an adjoining office. At the beginning of his tenure, March discovered that on Baker's desk was a buzzer that the secretary could press when he wanted the chief of staff. The first time Baker pressed it, March pulled out the buzzer's wire.

What had all this to do with President Wilson? The most obvious connection, as mentioned, was the president's quixotic appointment of an
erstwhile student. Having made this mistake, the president should have
watched the result and taken measures to remove Baker from the war
department. Instead, the president took every occasion to protect Baker.
Colonel House, always deft and careful, especially when approaching the
president, suggested to Wilson before the beginning of the war that Baker
and his counterpart in the navy department, Secretary Josephus Daniels,
should be relieved. They were good men, he wrote in his diary, but good-
ness could be effective only in peacetime, and they "did not fit in with
war." The colonel thought they did not have public support and the mistakes they were sure to make would be laid upon the shoulders of the
president. He believed that Wilson had "taken a gamble that there would
be no war and had lost" and must deal with the needs of a war administration. To all this, or something close to it, the president "listened with a
kindly and sympathetic attention and while he argued with me upon many
of the points, he did it dispassionately."[15]

The most remarkable testimony to Wilson's judgment in supporting
Baker came some years later, in 1929, and Baker in innocence made it
himself. The former secretary, back in Cleveland, wrote Pershing's former
supply officer, Major General James G. Harbord, that "I think the world
and you would be very much surprised indeed if you could realize how
completely President Wilson let me run the War department without ever
an order, and with only the rarest suggestion, from him." Baker said he
tried to keep Wilson informed by reports, formal and otherwise, "but his
time was much taken up with other things and I frequently found it
difficult to keep him in touch with the larger activities of the department
much less the detail." He told Harbord that as far as selection of officers
was concerned, he did not consult the president about anything except the
appointment of Pershing and the refusal to allow Major General Leonard
Wood to go to France. He did give the president the lists of promotions
to general officer, but that information was required as the president had
to nominate general officers to the Senate.[16]

In examining the Wilson war department in 1917–1918 one turns finally
to the army's first two wartime chiefs of staff, Scott and Bliss, as much mis-
fits in their office as were the secretary of war and his chief, the president.

How the president could have tolerated them is difficult to comprehend, other than by the fact that Wilson himself was so unwarlike, so unimpressed, even repelled, by the work of war.

The case of Scott is alarming. He appears to have received the rank of brigadier general because after Wilson's inauguration in 1913 the president asked General Wood, then chief of staff, if he, as president, had the authority to appoint a general. Wood said he did. The president thereupon promoted Scott, whose brother had been a member of the faculty at Princeton and supported Wilson during disputes with the faculty over student membership in the eating clubs and the organization of the graduate school. Having attained general officer rank by preferment, Scott managed to become chief of staff. He was troubled with sleepiness. Secretary of the Interior Franklin K. Lane wrote privately in February 1917 that at a meeting Scott fell asleep—"Mars and Morpheus in One!" Scott knew little about the war. He asked a colonel on his staff, Robert E. Lee Michie, about the Battle of the Marne. "Michie," he said, "everybody's talking about the Battle of the Marne. What happened at the Battle of the Marne anyway?"[17]

Baker liked Scott and described him fondly, although in 1918 under pressure from General March he concurred in Scott's relief from command of a training camp at Fort Dix, New Jersey. March and Baker had gone up to Dix and there listened while the general took forty-five minutes to describe the meaning of the feathers in an Indian warbonnet. Scott had been an Indian fighter in the old days and once had stood on a high peak with Captain Frederick Benteen, of Custer fame, and there they had seen herds of buffalo that filled the plains for twenty miles. Those had been Scott's good days. In 1917–1918 he should have been on the front porch of the Old Soldiers Home in Washington, D.C.[18] After the relief from Fort Dix, Scott's wife wrote Baker plaintively asking that her husband receive the four stars of a full general that had gone to Pershing, to March as chief of staff, and to Scott's successor as chief, Bliss.[19]

Tasker Bliss did not fit the war department's needs in 1917–1918 any more than did Scott, if for a different reason. Scott had written orders on little pads of paper, in a large, bold hand, a symbol of his inefficiency. Bliss in comparison was a scholar; he knew Greek and Latin and would have done well as a professor of classical languages and literature in a small college. Instead he seems to have believed that he could analyze not merely warfare but also international relations, although he had no experience in either. Robert L. Bullard, who became commander of the Second Army under Pershing and was one of the two officers to receive the rank of lieutenant general during the war, despised Bliss, who he said was a theorist with almost no experience with troops. As for the international analyses, Bliss later made them when he was one of the five American commissioners at the Paris Peace Conference. He wrote dozens of memorandums about foreign affairs in Europe and elsewhere, memos that President Wilson may not have read. But, to be sure, in the war department it did not matter if one wrote notes, as did Scott, or memorandums, as did Bliss. Neither officer was a sufficient mover of the bureaucracy; the extraordinary shuffling and paper passing disgraced the department during the first year of participation in World War I.[20]

3

As the year 1917 drew to an end, criticism of both economic and military mobilization began to be heard. The furies were gathering. Everything moved into a crisis, and, as commander in chief, President Wilson had to face the crisis.

Some of the criticism of the administration's handling of economic and military mobilization was personal and political. At the beginning of the war, former president Theodore Roosevelt had asked to lead a division, and the administration properly turned him down—Roosevelt was intellectually keen but physically worn, no longer the Rough Rider of 1898. His proposed division would have drawn off the best officers the army possessed, which Baker and Wilson could not have allowed. His commissioning as a major general would have ruined the decision of the war department to appoint most field-grade officers for the line, majors and above, from the regular army. The result was that Roosevelt, who never liked "that skunk in the White House," went into opposition and soon was writing editorials published and syndicated by the *Kansas City Star* that were increasingly critical of the slowness—he used other words—of the Washington leadership.

There was a personal element about the criticism, and yet it was more than that. Wilson and Baker watched the criticism mount and consoled themselves—and believed it was true—that the critics were inspired by personal and Republican irritation. But mobilization had been so poorly handled that the critics had much more in mind. Senator Henry Cabot Lodge expressed their feeling when he wrote Lord Bryce, "The fact is that the president has no administrative capacity. He lives in the sunshine. He wants nobody to tell him the truth apparently and he has a perfect genius for selecting little men for important places."[21] The critics had tired of Denman and his argument with Goethals, would have been outraged over the president's treatment of Pierre Du Pont had they known of it, and were exasperated by Baker and Scott and Bliss. When Roosevelt criticized the president he undoubtedly had himself in mind as civil head of a new administration and General Wood in mind for the war department. Many critics would have supported such changes, and the combination might have led to accomplishment—what a combination they might have been in wartime Washington!

At the beginning of the crisis over mobilization the president's opponents chose to focus not on Wilson, although the target was tempting, but on the war department. The president could exert the power of his office against critics however well informed, but Baker and Scott and Bliss had no such protection. It was easier to take on the war department than the war economy, a scattered proposition compared to the war department, which was concentrated in the State, War, and Navy Building next to the White House.

The department was in saddening shape. Its administrative apparatus, its bureau system, had broken down. Secretary John C. Calhoun had created the system after the War of 1812, placing each activity of the department in a bureau, and by the Wilson administration a general known as a chief headed each bureau. The system had collapsed before, during the war against Spain in 1898, when the army put into Cuba in the vicinity of Santiago a force smaller than a single division under Pershing's command in France.

During the presidential administration of William H. Taft, General Wood had sought to enforce reforms sponsored by Secretary of War Elihu Root, but the chiefs were long accustomed to maneuvering, and they soon bounded back when an act of Congress in 1916 stipulated that no officer of the general staff could hold an administrative post. Baker accepted this attenuation of the authority of Generals Scott and Bliss, which perhaps was not a bad idea, but the result when war was declared was that the department was again operating as a fragmented organization, each chief doing what seemed right in his own eyes. Baker compounded the situation by giving each chief what amounted to a hunting license to search out and obtain, or make contracts for, scarce supplies. After the war a war department colonel wrote that the result was a "slowing down" that almost paralyzed the department in the winter of 1917–1918. An official study of army administration later excoriated the bureau system and Baker's part in enlarging its inefficiencies. Baker "had had little contact with the management of large-scale enterprises where the necessity for firm executive control was taken for granted. . . . Without effective leadership the war department bumped its way from one crisis to another toward disaster."[22]

At this juncture a combination of an act of God and an act by the administration brought the crisis. The war economy was creaking along, not getting far; Pershing had been in France for six months and received four of the thirty divisions Baker promised. Then the winter of 1917–1918 turned appallingly cold, the worst in fifty years, minus twenty degrees in Boston, minus sixteen in Albany. There were two huge snowstorms. On January 5, 1918, winds of fifty-five miles an hour brought the first, a fifteen-inch snowfall that blocked railroad terminals around the country. The second storm struck six days afterward. Then came one of the most inept orders by a federal administrative official in the twentieth century, perhaps since 1789. The president in his mobilization effort had appointed a Princeton colleague and later president of Williams College, Harry A. Garfield, son of the assassinated president, as head of the Fuel Administration. Garfield found a perfect mess, which in fact had been caused by the president himself. Wilson had fixed the price of bituminous coal at two dollars a ton, when a price of three was necessary to keep marginal mines in operation. Production losses began late in the summer of 1917, and by December production was down by six million tons a month. At that time, when almost all energy was produced by coal—for houses, factories, and ships—the loss produced a coal crisis. Ships were unable to leave eastern ports, and freight cars full of war materiel piled up from eastern harbors to Pittsburgh. Matters became so critical that the army used ships for storage. Garfield appears to have had no guidance, and on January 16, the coal crisis upon him, ordered a five-day embargo on the use of coal in almost all factories east of the Mississippi, beginning the next day, after which nonessential industry was to go to a five-day week, shutting for nine "heatless Mondays" from January 28 until March 25.

The storm that burst upon the administration was one of the two crises of Wilson's presidency, the other being the controversy with the Senate over the League of Nations. It was fortunate for the president that only after the coal shortage did the economic cost become evident—in lost wages and production the coal embargo cost an estimated $4.3 billion; a coal journal calculated that it saved 3.4 million tons, but measured against losses the cost per ton was $1,256.94. People sensed this disaster, if they did not know the details. Senator George E. Chamberlain of Oregon, chairman of the committee on military affairs and a Democrat, spoke in New York and called for a cabinet minister of munitions. Realizing that such a secretary would be dominated by the other cabinet secretaries, he amended a bill to that effect to propose a war cabinet or council of "three distinguished citizens of demonstrated ability" to function independently of the cabinet, directly under the president, with almost unlimited control of the war, economic and military preparations alike. Had the bill passed, it would have taken direction of the war out of President Wilson's hands.

All the while the critics were moving toward Baker, demanding his resignation. Criticism turned savage, people saying the country needed a butcher, not a Baker. Colonel George Harvey of *Harvey's Weekly,* once a Wilson supporter, discovered that if one rearranged the letters of Baker's name it spelled BRAKE. Colonel House—no more a colonel than Harvey but still a Wilson supporter—did not know what to do about Baker, whom he had tried to get out of office nearly a year before. A month earlier he had suggested that Baker might become private secretary to the president, but that raised in Wilson's mind the question of his own loyalty to Joseph P. Tumulty, the secretary who had been with him since his governorship of New Jersey. The Texas colonel wrote in his diary that everything was in chaos and Baker did not realize its seriousness. "He does not at all appreciate the fact that everyone who knows the situation in Washington has lost confidence in the organization." And how to tell the president? "Neither does the president appreciate this, so there you are."[23]

House always believed that his influence on the president varied with the subject; in foreign affairs, the president would probably accept House's advice, but in domestic matters he would listen and do nothing. House was highly unsure of his ability to change domestic arrangements, yet, somehow, when we piece together what House wrote in his diary and Baker's subsequent actions, it appears to have been House who resolved the crisis over economic and military mobilization. House talked with Baker and may have stirred the secretary to the action that saved the day.[24]

Beginning on January 12, 1918, the secretary had testified before the Senate military affairs committee, for four days, but after talking with House he went before the committee a second time, on January 28, speaking for four and a half hours, and by all testimony did so with success. According to Senator Reed Smoot, Republican of Utah and no supporter of the president, "all agreed it was a fine presentation of a very poor case." A British diplomat in Washington not altogether friendly to his American hosts wrote Foreign Secretary Arthur Balfour that the secretary of war had done well, giving "a masterly performance." The newspaperman David Lawrence, another of Wilson's former students, at Princeton, sent the president an enthusiastic note saying he had just come from the Capitol after listening to Baker, and his presentation had been a masterpiece of convincing description.[25] The secretary had said that although General Pershing had few divisions at the moment he would have a million and a half men by the end of the year and America's soldiers would have all the equipment they needed.

The president, too, like Baker, was now showing steel. Senator Henry F. Ashurst of Arizona, a Democratic enthusiast to be sure, wrote in his diary that he "called upon W.W. and found him in a fighting mood. His jaw was set. His eyes shot fire."[26] The president said publicly that Senator Chamberlain's charges were "astonishing and absolutely unjustified distortions of the truth."

Then two more chance events intervened, this time in the president's favor. Roosevelt was hospitalized for a serious illness, and a similar affliction took Senator Chamberlain out of the fray. The president in his own hand wrote out a bill that became the Overman Act, conferring virtually dictatorial powers upon himself to organize and direct the nation's resources. Public opinion may have begun to tire of all the accusation, and there were suggestions in the press that a few speechless days on Capitol Hill would help win the war as much as heatless days imposed by the Fuel Administration.

The administration made two brilliant moves. On the side of economic mobilization the president on March 4 appointed Baruch chairman of the War Industries Board. Almost at the same time Baker brought General March back from France, where he had been Pershing's chief of artillery, to be chief of staff of the army. During the months of war that remained Baruch did what was possible, mainly a rewriting of war department orders, and by voluntary measures—to which he gave the appearance both of patriotism and of immense power, even though he did not possess it— brought some order into war production. March took on the Baker-Scott-Bliss war department and turned it upside down, doing a magnificent job in snatching order out of chaos.[27]

A triumphant outcome is not a fitting conclusion to any measurement of President Wilson as commander in chief during the first major foreign war the United States fought. Looking back on 1917–1918 from the vantage of a new century, the historian cannot help but conclude that blame for the errors in mobilization, economic and military, should lie with the commander in chief. The responsibility was Wilson's, if behind it was the confidence of the Victorian era, his dogmatic hatred of war, and his successes as a university professor.

Three

WARREN G. HARDING'S
REPUTATION

T HE ESSAY that follows necessarily omits several aspects of the decline and fall of President Harding's reputation. Here it is impossible to set out the whispering that arose over his sudden death in San Francisco, which the five physicians in attendance, including the then president and a former president of the American Medical Association, pronounced as the result of a stroke, but was obviously caused by a heart attack—a stroke requires at least ten minutes before death, and Harding died within seconds. Shortly afterward the talk arose that the president might have been poisoned, this because his personal physician, Dr. Charles E. Sawyer, injudiciously remarked to the press the possibility that Harding ate some spoiled crabmeat left over from his Alaska visit. This possibility the writer Samuel Hopkins Adams elaborated in a novel of 1926, entitled *Revelry,* about a mythical president who was poisoned. In 1927 a graduate of the Marion, Ohio, high school, Nan Britton, who had known Harding slightly and studied with the president's sister, who was her English teacher, published a long book, *The President's Daughter,* about her own daughter, conceived out of wedlock, whom she claimed was Harding's daughter. There was good reason to believe that in writing the book Ms. Britton enjoyed the skilled assistance of a former Presbyterian and Methodist minister who had become a public relations man and then a publisher of editions of the

Bible, Richard Wightman, for whom she was working as a secretary in New York. Three years later a former agent in the Bureau of Investigation, the predecessor of the Federal Bureau of Investigation in the department of justice, Gaston B. Means, arranged for a book that he did not write, which his ghostwriter later repudiated in entirety, *The Strange Death of President Harding,* that claimed the dead president's wife had poisoned her husband. These developments literary, sexual, and medical-literary, were enough to destroy a presidential reputation.

All the while, in veiled fashion before the president's death but revealed in detail shortly thereafter, came three scandals—one should say the appearance of scandals, for the most part—that filled the nation's newspapers. One was a case of bribery in the Veterans' Bureau, presided over by a venal appointee, Charles R. Forbes, whom the president at the urging of his wife had appointed. Harding was taking steps to settle this instance of small-time bribery when his cross-country tour of 1923, followed by a visit to Alaska, placed too much of a burden on his serious cardiac illness—the president's systolic blood pressure at the time of his inauguration in 1921 was 180. A second scandal developed months after the president's death when it became apparent that his former secretary of the interior, Albert B. Fall, a former senator whom the Senate had confirmed unanimously for his cabinet post, turned out to have taken several hundred thousands of dollars in loans, which he said were (and in his mind they seem to have been) in order to reduce his mortgages and improve his vast ranch properties in New Mexico. In return, it seemed, Fall gave two oilmen, Harry F. Sinclair and Edward L. Doheny, naval oil reserves in Elk Hills, California, and Teapot Dome in Wyoming. Last, the so-called Harding scandals (Democratic Party orators, scenting victory in the elections of 1924, so described them) involved a murky bank account held by Attorney General Harry M. Daugherty in the Washington Courthouse (Ohio) bank of his brother, allegedly for use in notorious briberies to make Harding president and keep the Harding administration afloat during its allegedly turbulent era in office. None of these scandals was very scandalous, compared with the long history of real-live scandals in almost every presidential administration during the history of the Republic. Except for the first, the malfeasance of Forbes, the president had no way of knowing about them, if in fact they existed.

But the whispering about murder and the claim of marital infidelity, together with the low-level or alleged scandals, thereafter combined with four other factors—Harding's ill fortune led to this—to destroy his reputation.]

1

Debunking—the word itself was amusing and believable—had long been an attractive part of American political life and filled a useful role, for when American politicians were inclined to stand upon their soapboxes and like the White Queen in *Through the Looking Glass* believe (in their cases relate) as many as six impossible things before breakfast every morning, unbelievers invariably called attention to the silly remarks. What distinguished the debunkers of the 1920s was the savagery behind the debunking—there was something venomous about it, a dislike that went beyond the horizons of humor, that was no simple using of funny occasions. The debunkers had what a later generation would describe as a hidden agenda. They did not like any American president of their generation and did not mind if they tore reputations to shreds, in gentlemanly prose if possible, in humor if that suited them, but with no real effort to search out the truth. Behind these tactics it might be said that they did not much like, not to mention admire, the American people, and considered democracy an impossible form of government.

One of the principal debunkers of the early 1920s was Clinton W. Gilbert, author of two books published in 1921 and 1922 by Putnam's in New York. They were entitled *The Mirrors of Washington* and *Behind the Mirrors: The Psychology of Disintegration at Washington.* The initial volume sold nearly one hundred thousand copies, so the second claimed. The successor may not have done so well, perhaps evidenced by the fact that no more such books appeared. The purpose of the books, apart from the theme revealed in the second volume's subtitle, was that a book, far more so than a newspaper article, would "scare a politician."[1] A book, Gilbert decided, or so his publisher wrote (on their title pages both books were anonymous), would bring not a smile nor a shrug but angry protest.

The style of the Gilbert books was careful, as the publisher's preface to the second related. The reason was not altogether convincing, but whoever wrote the preface (probably Gilbert) advanced it. A book should be "far less bitter, far more balanced," than a newspaper story. This said little for the prose of newspapers and was belied in the columns of many newspapers even of that perhaps less balanced journalistic era. The *Mirrors* books nonetheless so announced their appearance, and a reader of several generations later must allow that the prose of the books was careful and did not go to extremes.

The message was anything but careful, middle-of-the-road. The author had a point of view that was jaundiced and sour and seemed to say that American politics of the preceding generation and assuredly of the moment, the first years after the World War, had been a tissue of errors. Each of the presidents of the past twenty years—Theodore Roosevelt, Wilson (Gilbert considered Taft unworthy of mention), and Harding—had been unworthy of the country. When Roosevelt was in the White House he gave a cachet to his time. He made himself the image of his fellow Americans, or they of him—this point did not seem clear to Gilbert. The Typical American (the capital was the author's) was "gay, robustious, full of the joy of living, an expansive spirit from the frontier, a picaresque twentieth century middle class Cavalier." This American hit the line hard, and without flinching. His laugh "shook the skies." Then came Wilson, and the Typical American had trouble with his soul. With roots in his churchgoing past, he carried the banner of the Lord, democracy, and idealism. He voted for Prohibition and suffrage for women. He was a Round Head in a Ford. Then, after eight years of this nonsense, the Typical American brought in "Warren Gamaliel Harding of the modern type, the Square Head." Harding's artistic taste was the movies. The postwar president found mental satisfaction in the "vague inanities" of the small-town newspaper. He put his faith in America, liberty, virtue, happiness, prosperity, and law and order, distrusting anything new except mechanical inventions.[2]

Before 1914 there was belief in Progress, and two beliefs followed. In the Progressive era the Typical American had paid five cents to ride the streetcar and hoped it might be three. Hope lay in the ideas of people of that time, which exposed businessmen and other unethical individuals for the trifling people they were; it was an era in which Americans could hope for new things; President Roosevelt was sure that during his administration, and for a short while that of his friend Taft, they would arrive, not in due time but in Republican time. Then the Democrats took over, and President Wilson instructed his fellowmen to believe not in Progress but in Man. The cost of streetcars did not go down but up, to (in 1922) seven or eight cents. The Great War was society's effort to compensate for the idea of evolution, of Progress. Man "wanted to show what he could do, in spite of his slimy origin." During the war, governments performed the impossible, even taking in hand the industrial mechanism that ordinarily was left to the control of "the forces," those inanimate objects that moved society. With the successful end of the war, Americans half suspected that they might be able to do the impossible in peace. Instead, although they did not know it, the war had broken the picture in their heads. In their uncertainty they did not know whether to put their money on Man or on Progress, "so we put it on Mr. Harding."[3]

Harding, in the mind of the author of the *Mirrors* books, was a sure example of confusion, for like the Typical American he did not know what to believe. He had come to manhood in the 1880s (Harding was born in 1865), when God was in heaven and the United States was surpassing Great Britain and Germany in steel production. From this perception of order Harding, like the Typical American, shifted to Progress under President Roosevelt. He echoed the phrases of belief in Man announced by President Wilson—the Brotherhood of Man, War to End War, and "We must be just even to those to whom we do not wish to be just." Then "some monstrous hand had turned the page and there was Harding," who knew no more than his countrymen.[4]

By his very background Harding was no individual to change anything. His mental atmosphere, comfortable as it was, was naught but that of a small town. His public experience before coming to Washington was brief service in the Ohio legislature and a term as lieutenant governor. His service in the U.S. Senate was short, beginner's work. He left no mark on legislation, and if he had retired at the end of his term his name would have existed only in the congressional directories, like that of a thousand others. As a public speaker he said nothing anyone could remember. He passed through the Great War and left no mark on it. He shared in the fierce debate about the League of Nations and the Treaty of Versailles, and it was possible to recall small personages such as Senators Porter J. McCumber of North Dakota, Frank B. Kellogg of Minnesota, George H. Moses of New Hampshire, and Medill McCormick of Illinois, all of whom said some things in the Senate's discussions, but no one recalled Harding. He sometimes said he had made a great speech, but no newspaper thought fit to publish it.

If during his presidential administration, which had just begun when Gilbert's books were published, Harding was in doubt about anything, which was unlikely, he still would do nothing. He would consult the "best minds" endlessly (he had used this phrase to characterize the members of his cabinet). He would consult business minds outside the cabinet. He would consult party opinion, though nothing could come from that. "His party has no opinion, it exists by virtue of its capacity to think nothing about everything and thus avoid dissensions." He would use his tact, of which he possessed a great deal, for it was his primary quality to find a solution, but the task would be essentially hopeless. A friend had said that "Warren is the best fellow in the world. He has wonderful tact. He knows how to make men work with him and how to get the best out of them. He is politically adroit. He is conscientious. He has a keen sense of his responsibilities. He has unusual common sense." The friend named other similar virtues. "Well, I asked him, 'What is his defect?' 'Oh,' he replied, 'the only trouble with Warren is that he lacks mentality.'"[5]

The author of *Mirrors* was saying that the country, the Typical American, had voted for nothing in government in Washington save "an immense inertia." And having defined total inactivity, Gilbert gave some advice to his readers. "The only thing to do is to laugh. You have trouble laughing? Look about you and you will find plenty to laugh at. Look at your President and laugh. Look at your Supreme Court and laugh. Not one of them knows whether he is coming or going."[6]

Gilbert, one might conclude, was a gentlemanly debunker, who wrote in measured periods, and even if he drew caricatures they did not puncture balloons and assault political reputations in the manner that his contemporary in debunking, Henry L. Mencken, did. There was a large difference in method.

Mencken had the same disdain for American politics as did the author of the *Mirrors* books. To him, politics was hopeless. He avowed that the presidents of the United States in the past thirty or forty years—he was more expansive than Gilbert—had done nothing for the sum of human knowledge. Their ideas had not enriched that sum. "On the contrary, most of these great men have discharged little save piffle."[7]

Like Gilbert, the Sage of Baltimore made the same appraisals of Presidents Roosevelt and Wilson, and the readers of his columns in the *Baltimore Sun,* and the many readers across the country whose newspapers reprinted the columns, did not have to use much imagination to sense what he was going to say about Harding. Roosevelt he liked in an inverted, roundabout way. He admired his "daily mountebankery," if only because it kept the ball in the air.[8] In T.R.'s day it was a pleasure to read the newspapers. Roosevelt, to be sure, was a bogus progressive. He was a maker of white protestations and black acts. His were bold stratagems and duplicities, sacrifice of faith and principle to the main chance, displaying "magnificent disdain of fairness and honor." But all this was better than what followed, which were weekly appendixes to the Revelation of Saint John the Divine. Wilson was a bogus liberal. He was "the Anglomaniacal Woodrow." Dr. Wilson's so-called ideals were sickening, from the initial time he "loosed his first evangelical dithyrambs upon the world." Woodrow came home from Paris in 1919 ranking with the masterminds of the ages. Writing on October 4, 1920, about the then president of the United States, Mencken observed that "he is now regarded by everyone save a despairing band of last-ditch fanatics as a devious and foolish fellow, of whom the nation will be well rid on March 4."[9]

Mencken did not look forward to what was going to happen on the first Tuesday in November 1920. On July 28 he related his reasoning, that the presidency tended, year by year, as democracy was perfected, to represent, more and more closely, the inner soul of the people. "We move toward a lofty ideal. On some great and glorious day the plain folks of the land will reach their heart's desire at last, and the White House will be adorned by a downright moron."[10] After Roosevelt and Wilson, the American people naturally were ready for a change. No sane American believed in any official statement of policy, foreign or domestic, having been fooled too often, callously and impudently. Whenever an idea roused him to enthusiasm and passion, its propounder dragged him into the mud and made it evil and disgusting. The average American in 1920 hence wanted a change. "He wants a renaissance of honesty—even of ordinary, celluloid politician's honesty. Tired to death of intellectual charlatanry, he turns despairingly to honest imbecility."[11]

In sorting out what was about to happen, the Sage did not think it mattered if the average American voted for a Democrat or for a Republican.

This had been proved in the recent war. Every time a Democratic patriot, capitalist or toiler, obtained an easy dollar at Hog Island, a Republican patriot would receive another dollar. Every time a German factory was sold for ten cents on the dollar to a deserving Democrat, a German mill went for eleven cents on the dollar to a Republican "full of exalted rage against the Hun."[12]

As for Senator Harding, who became the Republicans' choice for the presidency at Chicago that summer, there was little that Harding could have done, if he was reading Mencken's columns, other than anticipate the worst from the Baltimore critic of American politics, which soon came; as a candidate he had to grit his teeth. Mencken predicted as early as February 9, 1920, that Harding was a second-rate provincial. Gleaming through this preliminary analysis was a belief that Ohio was run by the Anti-Saloon League, and this if nothing else turned the critic against the man he soon was describing as "Gamaliel." By July 26, with Harding in place to win—his nomination meant his election, as Mencken well knew, given the extraordinary anti-Wilson feeling after the defeat of the league and the treaty—the analysis hardened. Harding "is simply a third-rate political wheel-horse, with the face of a moving-picture actor, the intelligence of a respectable agricultural implement dealer, and the imagination of a lodge joiner."[13]

Mencken voted for Harding. That, to be sure, as he described it to his readers, was an ordeal, upon which he loosed his choicest invective. It was Mencken at his best, and smiles and laughter must have reverberated around the living rooms of Baltimore and wherever Mencken's columns were read:

> After meditation and prayer of excessive virulence for many days and consultation with all the chief political dowsers of the Republic, I conclude with melancholy that God lays upon me the revolting duty of voting for the numskull, Gamaliel, on the first Tuesday in November. It is surely no job to lift the blood pressure and fill the liver with hosannahs. Since I acquired the precious boon of the suffrage, in the year 1901, I have never had to cast my vote for a worse dub. The hon. Gentleman is an almost perfect specimen of a 100% American right-thinker. The operations of his medulla oblongata (the organ, apparently, of his ratiocination) resemble the rattlings of a colossal linotype charged with rubber stamps.[14]

He did not let well enough alone. On November 1 he opened his column with "Tomorrow the dirty job. I shall be on my knees all night."[15]

The columnist may have voted for Harding because he anticipated four years of throwing brickbats at Harding the orator and surely was disappointed when he received the opportunity for only two and one-half. He had published *The American Language* in 1919 and would follow that classic with two supplements. Anyone who has read around in the books— they sometimes read like telephone books, enormous compilations of words and meanings, note cards beyond belief—can see how Harding's oratory, however short the opportunity, was in for a bath. A century earlier, Mencken had written, the nation had experienced the Jacksonians, who came to power after the Republic's founders believed they, the fathers, had expressed the nation's soul in precise, intelligent eighteenth-century words, dedicated to an age when a word meant what it said. He obviously anticipated that history would repeat itself. The Jacksonians, he wrote in *The American Language,* lived in an era when newspapers suddenly multiplied and people everywhere were hungry for news, and unfortunately in Congress there was almost no business, nothing to talk about so it would fill up the newspapers. So the country's "corn-fed etymologists" filled out the language by placing adjectives and adverbs before every noun and verb and by pulling out nouns with suffixes such as "ation" and turning good nouns into verbs by adding "ize." The result was a horror that people for the rest of the century had to endure while trying, if it was possible, to sweep back the waters. Some progress had been made. But then with the advent of Roosevelt, Wilson, and then, horror of horrors, Harding, the nation's prose was bound to be ruined for another century. It would be Mencken's self-appointed task this time to sweep back the waters.

The writer hoped that the sheer exercise of Harding's style in his speeches, some of which he believed had shown clarity and vigor, would help the Ohioan pick up facility in writing. After all, writing was easy, "a trivial art, and well within the capacities of any normal adult with sufficient patience." He believed writing to be a literary gift valuable to a politician, "particularly if it take the form of a talent for mere words, as opposed to ideas."

But then came the inaugural speech. On "the question of the logical content of Dr. Harding's harangue of last Friday" he confessed to confusion. The president had said that the United States entered the late war

because of a "concern for preserved civilization." He presumed that Harding should be "holding down the chair of history in some American university." When the orator remarked that "ours is a constitutional freedom
where the popular will is supreme, and minorities are sacredly protected,"
he remembered the "Red scare" after the war, abandoned himself to mirth,
and sent picture postcards of Wilson's last attorney general, Mitchell
Palmer, and of the Atlanta penitentiary, at that time still the home of
Eugene Debs, to all of his enemies who happened to be socialists. As for
the words in which Harding clothed his ideas, "When Dr. Harding pre-
pares a speech he does not think it out in terms of an educated reader
locked up in jail, but in terms of a great horde of stoneheads gathered
around a stand."

> I rise to pay my small tribute to Dr. Harding. Setting aside a college
> professor or two and half a dozen dipsomaniacal newspaper reporters,
> he takes the first place in my Valhalla of literati. That is to say, he
> writes the worst English that I have ever encountered. It reminds me
> of a string of wet sponges; it reminds me of tattered washing on the
> line; it reminds me of stale bean-soup, of college yells, of dogs bark-
> ing idiotically through endless nights. It is so bad that a sort of gran-
> deur creeps into it.[16]

The amusing thing about Harding's inaugural address was that Harding
did not write it. It was written by one of his advisers, a professor of political economy at Johns Hopkins University—in Mencken's home city.

The speech moved Mencken to yearn for "the sweeter song, the rubber-
stamps of more familiar design, the gentler and more seemly bosh of the
late Woodrow."[17]

According to Mencken, Harding had no purpose in life other than to
be reelected. When Attorney General Daugherty in the spring of 1923
announced that Harding was a candidate for reelection, Mencken announced that it was certainly not news, that the plain fact was that Harding became an active candidate for a second term at 12:01 p.m. on March 4,
1921. When Harding died, and newspapers said he had passed on because
of the intolerable cares and burdens of the presidential office, the columnist observed that at the time Harding collapsed he was not engaged in
presidential duties but in a canvass for renomination and reelection.

In observing the president of 1921–1923, Mencken touched every field of Harding's endeavor, including foreign policy. He declared himself in favor of the League of Nations because, although he regarded it as "thumpingly dishonest," like democracy it deserved to be tried.[18] Within a few years its principal members would be trying to slaughter one another. When Harding came out for American membership in the World Court, the critic declared it would edge the United States into the league, for the court was only the league in a new false face, with the Union Jack concealed beneath the undershirt.

In January 1924 the columnist together with George Jean Nathan and the publisher Alfred Knopf founded the *American Mercury,* with the duty "to track down some of the worst nonsense prevailing and to do execution upon it."[19] In its first year the *Mercury's* every issue contained at least one disparaging remark about Harding. First it was Mencken's description of the "funeral orgies," which spared nothing. "No man ever passed into the Eternal Vacuum to the tune of more delicious rhetoric." The account related the "ghastly progress" of the funeral train as it passed "that double file of village mayors, newspaper photographers, scared school children and anonymous morons," who gurgled, sniffed, choked, and moaned. As the Teapot Dome hearings filled the newspapers, the *Mercury* collected and quoted such obituary remarks as that of the *Bookman,* that Harding was "the most thoroughly trusted by the people at large of any President of our time." Bishop William E. Anderson of Cincinnati had quoted Harding as saying, "My prime motive in going to the White House is to bring America back to God." The Kiwanis Club magazine's tribute caught the eye of the *Mercury:*

> Oh, Son of God — to God returned —
> Peace to thee with a rest well earned,
> Thy gentle face and quiet calm
> Remains to us a golden balm.

For the *Mercury* the problem thereafter became how to memorialize President Harding, and a two-page editorial noted the work of the Harding Memorial Association. What, specifically, could it do? Erect an equestrian statue of the Martyr in Marion? Place hand-painted oil paintings of him in all the far-flung halls of the Benevolent and Protective Order of

Elks? Endow a Brig. Gen. Charles E. Sawyer chair of homeopathy in the Johns Hopkins Medical School?

Mencken's political judgment, let it be added, was as poor as his prose was bright. Indeed, it was not merely poor; it was terrible. Consider his judgment in the presidential year of 1924, when the Democratic Party nearly committed suicide in nominating the Wall Street lawyer John W. Davis on the 103d ballot, all this in Madison Square Garden, which in those days was not air-conditioned. When this absurdity of politics and physical endurance took place, Mencken had no idea what was going on. Somewhere near the end of the casting of ballots he sat down before his Corona portable and wrote the following lead for a story in the *Baltimore Sun:* "Everything is uncertain in this convention but one thing: John W. Davis will never be nominated." Told that Davis was nominated shortly after he filed his story, the reporter was stunned for a moment and said, "Why that's incredible! I've already sent off a story that it's impossible." Then as an afterthought: "I wonder if those idiots in Baltimore will know enough to strike out the negative."[20] That year Mencken pronounced Davis a liar, Coolidge a prospect worse than Harding, and voted for the hopeless Robert M. LaFollette.

2

Late in the 1920s books by journalists began to appear, each representing Harding's presidency as a time of great presidential weakness, and no one was more dedicated to that interpretation than William Allen White, who was first in the field, in 1928, with *Masks in a Pageant,* a survey or run-through of the presidents he had known beginning with Benjamin Harrison and ending with Coolidge. He included an utterly malicious interpretation of Harding.

Any explanation of why White took such a stance must of course include his incurable, inoperable worship of the late President Roosevelt, who had passed on in 1919 and who if he had lived would undoubtedly have taken the Republican nomination in 1920. White once wrote, "Roosevelt bit me, and I went mad." He never forgot that day in December 1918 when he saw Roosevelt for the last time, ill in Roosevelt Hospital in New

York. It is easily understandable therefore that when Harding received the nomination in 1920, White remembered sadly his old friend who had died. He especially would have remembered that the Ohio politician turned his back on the great T.R. by helping renominate President Taft in 1912, instead of giving the nomination to Roosevelt, who had broken with Taft and wanted another presidential term for himself. Harding was a party regular and refused to have anything to do with a party split. The same was not true of Roosevelt, who defied the regulars and took his followers to another hall in Chicago, let them march around singing "Onward, Christian Soldiers," and allowed them to create the Progressive Party that became better known from his own wondrous remark, "I feel like a bull moose." To White it did not matter that Roosevelt's candidacy in 1912 divided the Republican Party and gave the election to the Democratic candidate, Wilson. The only thing that mattered was that the regulars including Harding had thwarted Roosevelt.

In White's view Harding's first error was that he was not Roosevelt and had acted against Roosevelt, and there may well have been a second—namely, that Harding like White had been a small-town newspaper editor. Years later the historian Randolph C. Downes received a letter from a correspondent containing a shrewd appraisal. "I always felt," Ben H. Mason opined, "that W. A. White never reconciled himself to the fact that a fellow editor made the White House and he didn't." He thought there was a vein of jealousy all through White's writings on Harding. White thought of himself as the spokesman for small-town editors, and "when the man from Marion came into sight, White was pushed into the background." White, he wrote, in memory of White's having backed Roosevelt and the Bull Moose candidacy in 1912, was a poor politician and a jealous editor.[21]

Curiously, in the campaign of 1920 (and by chance in opposition to another upstart small-town editor, James M. Cox, of Dayton, Ohio, who was the Democratic nominee), White backed Harding. It is true that White later wrote of himself at the Chicago convention as a "sad fat figure" toddling around the hall during the traditional uproar for Harding's nomination, while bands played, trumpets brayed, and the crowd howled.[22] But White did more to support Harding than get out on the floor. After the nomination he complimented the candidate in words that readers of *Masks in a Pageant* might have remembered, had they known of them.

"You are making a great impression on the American people," he wrote. "You have grown every moment since the day of the nomination. It seems to me that your sincerity, your sense of dignity and your steady thoughts have made themselves felt in the American heart."[23]

Then, not long after Harding died, White turned around and soon was thundering about Harding's iniquities. Apparently the reason was Teapot Dome, which to White was a terrible affair as he wrote about it in his book of 1928. Words could hardly describe his contempt. He mustered up his choicest phrases to describe how awful the scandal was. "Then slowly all the scandal which had been hidden came out, and with the truth, which was bad enough, came lies and innuendoes. Before scandal had reached him, men started to raise a memorial to him. A myth was born that he was a beloved president, a sweet and kindly man, like Lincoln. But— alas!—the myth was abortive. His friends, cronies, allies, and the Ohio gang were haled into court." The scandal reminded White of the Greek tragedy that all the youths of his era read about (Greek tragedy is no longer the stuff of modern education, no longer has any place in American political measurements). Without hesitation he scurried to ancient Athens to draw the scene:

> Always there must have been, in the dark periphery of his conscious-ness, cackling, ribald voices: Daugherty's voice, Fall's voice, drunken voices, raucous in debauch, the high-tensioned giggle of women pursued, the voices of men whispering in the greedy lechery of political intrigue; cynical voices cackling like the flames of the pit in scurrilous derision at the booming presidential rhetoric, Harding's high faluting yearnings. This was his hell; the hell which he could only escape by sinking further into it, and forgetting his lofty emprise. So fools rattled their heels in the White House and on the decks of the *Mayflower* while Harding relaxed.[24]

In *Masks,* White exhibited proof of Harding's knowledge of Teapot Dome. After the *Henderson* left Alaskan waters for Vancouver, he wrote, Harding received from Washington a long message in code, brought by seaplane. "This message clearly upset him. For a day or so he was near col-lapse. He recovered somewhat, but remained distraught and worried."[25] It was a good story, agreeable to imaginations of the time when seaplanes were on the pages of every Sunday newspaper in the glossy, sepia-colored rotogravure section. The story, however, never has had the slightest proof, the seaplane delivery never verified, the contents of a message, if delivered, never revealed.

The truth was that White's allegations reached a great deal farther than his evidence. Teapot Dome seems to have mesmerized him. "Rumor said," he wrote, "probably apocryphally" (which was hardly enough warning to a reader about the rumor he was spreading), that Harding signed over the oil reserves from Secretary of the Navy Edwin L. Denby to Fall when the president was drunk. He grasped for anything to criticize Harding: Daugherty's friend Jess Smith, "in the midst of his activities, under a threat, probably from the White House, of prosecution, killed himself— or was murdered by those whom his confessions might have involved."[26]

Reading the yellowing pages of *Masks in a Pageant,* library copies of which are torn and fragmented, corners bent where some student of old wished to remember a torrid passage, pages underlined in pencil and the fountain-pen ink of that time, one has the impression that White chose to pillory Harding for several reasons—devotion to Roosevelt, possibly the small-town-editor problem, perhaps Teapot Dome. And then there was something else, which could be described as a literary opportunity. White wrote privately to the Wilsonian reformer Brand Whitlock, the erstwhile mayor of Toledo, on July 15, 1926, that he was thinking of writing a biography of Harding. "If ever there was a man who was a he-harlot, it was . . . Warren G. Harding," he advised Whitlock. "But I suppose it ought not to be written now. It would hurt too many hearts. I don't know. I could write it, but it would be a bitter and awful thing."[27] Then late that year came publication of *Revelry,* and during the next year *The President's Daughter* was published; the time was right, and so White wrote his biography.[28]

Frederick Lewis Allen was not a journalist but editor of *Harper's,* and in *Only Yesterday,* published in 1931, he wrote not so much about Harding as about "the golden twenties." But his distortion of what happened during that decade was highly important for what people remembered, including college and university students of the 1930s and thereafter who read the book as collateral reading in their courses. That his book was a New Yorker's view of the United States passed completely over their heads; they did not recognize that across the length and breadth of what was a very large country most Americans not merely never saw but never even heard of much of what Allen passed off as American history. Moreover, when the editor of *Harper's* described the Harding era he treated it as a journalist might have, stressing sensational events. As Robert K. Murray has cataloged his treatment, he devoted four pages to the Harding administration's constructive activities—including two lines to the peace treaty with Germany in 1921, seven to creation of the Bureau of the Budget giving the country a careful budget for the first time in its national existence, one line to the tariff that was a serious issue after World War I, six lines to tax policy that was even more important, four lines on war debts and reparations, and four on labor problems. He gave twenty-two pages to the Harding scandals.[29]

Four years after White's book, a year after Allen's, there appeared a far different production, a scholarly article on Harding by Allan Nevins in the *Dictionary of American Biography,* half a dozen double-column pages; it deserves inclusion in the works of Harding journalism because its origin was as political and personal as was that of the Harding pages in *Masks in a Pageant,* the result almost as irresponsibly trivial as the pages of *Only Yesterday.*[30] As White was a Rooseveltian Republican, so Nevins worshipped at the shrine of the late President Wilson. Nevins had been a graduate student at the University of Illinois when Wilson became president and could not forget his hero, the gallant fighter for a new world order who went down to defeat before the malevolent senators who mainly for reasons of regular Republican politics defeated the League of Nations Covenant. How could he forget the leather-lunged Republican, William E. Borah of remote Idaho, who had never been out of the United States and never would go out of the United States and who claimed to be a Progressive but always wandered back to regularity? Or the elegant Boston Brahmin, Henry Cabot Lodge, a Harvard graduate who once said of a Wilson speech that it might get by at Princeton but not at Harvard?

Nevins had another reason for hating Harding. The present writer remembers vividly seeing Nevins give his presidential address to the American Historical Association and hearing him tell his auditors how in his early years as a newspaperman, before he became a historian in the 1920s and taught first at Cornell University and then for the rest of his long life at Columbia University, he had worked for the Dayton editor Cox, whom

Harding defeated. Nevins idolized Cox, almost as much as he did Wilson. Harding defeated Cox by an enormous majority of fourteen million votes to eight million. Cox had gone down the line for Wilson's league and met ignominious defeat.

From these two points of view of Wilson and Cox, which were likely to produce a distorted result, not much different, one reinforcing the other, Nevins came at his presidential sketch of Harding. But another factor entered the equation that ensured error, guaranteeing that the sketch would lack any distinction: it was too soon to make a considered judgment because of the unavailability of source material—such as the Harding papers, then languishing in Marion. Here probably was an error of the *Dictionary* for which he wrote. The *Dictionary* was a grand project to do definitive short biographies of American subjects and was sponsored by an impeccable group of learned societies, its editorial board filled by the finest historians of the time, but an earlier cap should have been put on the subjects considered in the twenty large initial volumes, probably the year 1900, instead of the cap placed on them, which was the requirement that subjects must be dead. And so from Wilsonian principles and totally inadequate sources Nevins produced an apparently evenhanded biograph-ical sketch that grossly misestimated Harding yet passed for the accepted outlook for many years thereafter. He wrote, most unfairly (for what were his proofs?), that Harding as a youth possessed "some dissipated habits" and led the neighborhood blades in their amusements. As a senator he was "drinking a good deal and playing poker," and the source was none other than "White, *post,*" the Latin reference lending éclat to the point and indi-cating citation of *Masks* in the accompanying bibliography. Harding had a "limited range of ideas." Because Daugherty was "the head of the Ohio machine or 'gang'" and was on Harding's side, the die was cast, Harding nominated and elected. Nevins repeated White's allegation that Jess Smith died because of "his sudden suicide or murder." He said Harding found out about Teapot Dome from Mrs. Fall, his source being Senator Arthur Capper of Kansas, quoted by "White, *post,* p. 432; partially denied by Mrs. Fall." On return from Alaska the president received the long Washing-ton message in cipher, duly brought by seaplane, and was so disturbed that "for a day or so he was near collapse," and the source was "Ibid.," again meaning White. The historian concluded that Harding by cruel misfortune "was lifted"—the passive voice raised a question of who or what lifted him—to a post beyond his powers. Among Nevins's titles in the bibliography was *The President's Daughter.*

The next year Alice Roosevelt Longworth, daughter of the president of 1901–1909, published her reminiscences in *Crowded Hours.* Although her purpose was to relate up to the time of writing (she lived many more years) the life of the once beautiful young woman who was married in the White House to Representative Nicholas Longworth of Ohio, in the latter 1920s speaker of the House, and for whom was named the color of "Alice blue" and a song that endured for generations, this narrative of a prominent life was as journalistic as its less personal predecessors. She was ever the champion of her father, whom Harding opposed in 1912. She told how the Hardings celebrated the defeat of the league and the treaty in the Senate, for after the votes (there were three, one in November 1919, and the other two on the same day the following March) a merry group went out to the Edward McLean estate and enjoyed an impromptu supper of scrambled eggs, with Mrs. Harding cooking the eggs. The purpose was to show that the Hardings took the league and treaty lightly. So did her father, and Alice and Nick, but the idea was to point to the Hardings. In her vignette of the celebrations she also showed the future first lady cooking eggs, a mundane scene. Later came the appraisal of Harding the president, during which assessment she compared Harding's study on the White House second floor to a speakeasy: "the air heavy with tobacco smoke, trays with bottles containing every imaginable brand of whisky stood about, cards and poker chips ready at hand—a general atmosphere of waistcoat unbuttoned, feet on the desk, and the spittoon alongside." As for her conclusion about Harding: "I think every one must feel that the brevity of his tenure of office was a mercy to him and to the country. Harding was not a bad man. He was just a slob."[31]

It was all caricature, apart from the bad manners of criticizing one's host—Nick had been at Harding's poker sessions, whatever their proportions, and Alice, too, had been known to take a hand. It was unbelievable; if there was all that much liquor around, why did the assistant White House physician, Boone, who was on the second floor on far more occasions than Alice (whose familiarity ended in 1909), never observe such spectacles? Boone never saw a bottle in the White House. The daughter of Theodore Roosevelt, one suspects, may have inveighed against the liquor in knowledge that her own husband had been a hard drinker for years.[32] And Downes's correspondent, Mason, had another explanation about her opposition to Harding, namely that Alice Longworth "never got used to the fact that her husband never made the White House, but that a small town editor made it and to rub salt into the wound, an Ohio small town editor." If Ohio was to have another president—it was known as "the mother of presidents" (Grant, Hayes, Garfield, McKinley, Taft)—in her mind it should have been Nick.[33]

Another piece of journalism was Mark Sullivan's sixth and last volume of *Our Times,* published in 1935, and it again advanced an evaluation of Harding that was as critical as those of White, Allen, Nevins, and Longworth. Like White and Longworth, Sullivan was a Rooseveltian. In Sullivan's case dislike came also from what he picked up from Washington gossip in his role as a journalist. He scouted the capital and heard the stories, and on August 2, 1923, while Harding lay dying in San Francisco, he was informing his diary of an alleged Harding girlfriend, a Washington woman.[34] But another wellspring of his dissatisfaction was his close friend Herbert Hoover, who before Harding's death had been fond of the president but afterward disliked him. In San Francisco, Hoover conferred several times daily with the medical team and was treated like one of them and told the doctors they had to save Harding because he was the only man who could hold the Republican Party together. After Harding died and Hoover saw his body lying there in the sickroom, he came out of the presidential suite in tears. Shortly after the president's death Hoover told a group of engineers:

> When he came into responsibility as President he faced unprecedented problems of domestic rehabilitation. It was a time when war-stirred emotions had created bitter prejudices and conflict in thought. Kindly and genial, but inflexible in his devotion to duty, he was strong in his determination to restore confidence and secure progress. All this he accomplished through patient conciliation and friendly goodwill for he felt deeply that hard driving might open unhealable breaches among our people. We have all benefited by the success of his efforts.

Within weeks Teapot Dome changed Hoover's mind, and Sullivan recorded him as saying at a dinner party that "Harding got all his recreation . . .

sitting around playing poker and telling shady stories night after night. He said it was a strain for him to talk to me or [Secretary of State Charles E.] Hughes and he only did it when business required it but the others rested and amused him." It was a scurrilous appraisal, and Sullivan shared it.[35]

For Sullivan to find a principle about which to organize his Harding narrative was not difficult, and it was Nan Britton's book. In setting out Ms. Britton's points he said they were not his. Setting them out nonetheless brought them to the attention of readers, just as White passed on the rumor that Jess Smith was murdered. Suitably, in a footnote, the device of scholarship, he remembered what White artfully described as the primrose path—primroses were nearly required parts of the gardens of small-town America in the 1920s, and along their paths ardent young men took their ardent girlfriends. Sullivan talked at length with Daugherty and asked whether there was any "woman scrape" in Harding's life, and Daugherty said, "If there had been one Harding would have told me." The former attorney general, known for his quickness, subtracted from this utterance by adding, "I know there was never any woman scrape in my life." Sullivan pressed the issue, and the response was an epigram, "I never talk about dead men or living women." A long account of Teapot Dome gave Sullivan opportunity to relate that Jess Smith kept the account labeled "Jess Smith Extra No. 3." The conclusion Sullivan came to was that it was to pay off individuals involved in the late president's "woman trouble." He might have been right, had he ascribed the account's utility to the case of a Harding neighbor in Marion, Ohio, Carrie Phillips. Not knowing about her, he obviously was referring to Nan Britton.

He did not neglect Ms. Britton's fellow vilifier, Means. In another footnote he remembered crudely, in the racial metaphor of the time, a remark made to him by "a colored bootblack at the old Shoreham Hotel, the compromise he made between his native delicacy and his curiosity," as to whether Harding had been "bumped off."[36]

Sullivan like Mencken tagged Harding with making bad speeches and did it in his usual indirect way rather than following Mencken's procedure, which was an auto-da-fé. Harding one day, doubtless with a grin, had told the members of the White House press corps, which might have numbered six or eight reporters, that he liked to get out on the speech circuit and, as he put it, "bloviate." He thereby invented a word. ("Normalcy" was not his invention.) The other reporters had the decency not to push the point, save Sullivan, who saw an opportunity. Sullivan put the word in *Our Times*.[37]

Last among the journalists was Adams, and his contribution to the misrepresentation of Harding's personality and administration was to embody White's criticisms, as testified to by Allen, Nevins, Longworth, and Sullivan, in a single readable volume that became the accepted account of the Harding era.

Adams was a master at making an unfair point, as in the following, about Harding's reading:

> The fact is that Warren G. Harding was and remained an unread man. Books did not enter his scheme of life in any important sense. The magic and the music were alien to him. He cannot fairly be called illiterate, although some of his verbiage, when he strives to attain the impressive, furnishes a sad example of the grandiloquently inept. We shall find it later in his speeches. He was aware of it and sensitive to criticism on the point. No; he was not illiterate. But he was unliterate. Or perhaps pseudo literate would be the juster characterization.[38]

The author did not stop to let the reader sense that most political leaders, for that matter leaders of any sort, were outward-turning people who had little time for books. If they surrounded themselves with books, as did Franklin D. Roosevelt and Adlai E. Stevenson, the books were unread, for their owners did not have the time. A man who knew Roosevelt well wrote of him that he did not think Roosevelt ever read a book; a friend asked him about the well-known best-seller by Kathleen Winsor, *Forever Amber,* and the president said, with a grin, that he only had read the dirty parts. A friend of Stevenson was in the latter's house and looking at the book-filled library and instinctively knew that the governor had not read those books. Harry Truman, known as a man of books, sometimes went for years without reading very much. A Truman biographer, Jonathan Daniels, observed that Truman knew history of a sort that David S. Muzzey might have written. When Truman talked about Andrew Jackson it was from Marquis James, and for Thomas Jefferson he turned to Claude Bowers.

To relate Adams's points is to repeat those of his predecessors, whose books he often cited, as "On the same page Mr. Sullivan refers to a 'woman scandal.'" Adams cited a pamphlet by Professor William Estabrook Chancellor of the College of Wooster, which claimed that Harding possessed

Negro blood, as one of the factors during the convention of 1920 that might have defeated Harding's nomination. He did not say he believed it, nor did he refuse to believe it; it was a piece of evidence of some sort. Another piece of evidence in which he believed in all its detail was *The President's Daughter;* he related its explanations as fact. He employed stories and aphorisms if critical of his subject. George Washington—he recited the gibe—could not tell a lie, but Harding could not tell a liar. This mot he credited to one of Harding's friends. The three needs of the Republican Party were positions on the three Ts that spelled trouble: tariff, taxation, and treaties. In Adams's narrative the man who talked himself out of the three Ts was Harding. Robert Murray has aptly dismissed Adams's book as "the primary transmission belt by which all the various slanted accounts and oft-repeated myths were carried to later generations."[39]

The inventiveness of the journalists of the 1920s and 1930s was, one must say, surprising. When the able writers of those years ran out of information they took what lay at hand.

Their books were brought out by the leading publishing houses of New York and Boston. White's publisher was Macmillan, Allen's of course was Harper, Nevins's and Alice Longworth's and Sullivan's was Scribner's, Adams's was Houghton Mifflin. Their editors assisted with the books. When former attorney general Daugherty wrote irately to Adams's publisher, protesting the book's errors, Ferris Greenslet informed him, "The forthcoming work is entirely historical in purpose and method. In writing it, Mr. Adams has had the advantage, in addition to his own very thorough investigations, of the discoveries made during more than five years of research by the leading authority on the period, Professor Alderfer of Penna. State College." (Harold F. Alderfer was the author of an unpublished doctoral dissertation on Harding.) "The greatest pains have been taken," Greenslet explained, "to document and substantiate all factual statements and there is hardly a page that does not carry at the bottom footnote references to the sources and authorities used."[40]

Once published, the books displayed a staying power that was as surprising as their uncertain provenance. They passed into the canon of respectability. In 1963 Dr. Boone, who when it came to plays and whatever appeared on television and in *Time* did not believe in leaving sleeping dogs lie, wrote to CBS News about a portrayal of Mrs. Harding that he had seen and considered a marked perversion of the truth, to put the case mildly. The producer, Perry Wolff, wrote back that four sources had been consulted. One was *White House Profile: A Social History of the White House, Its Occupants and Its Festivities,* published by the newspaperwoman Bess Furman in 1951. The other three were the books of Allen, Longworth, and Adams. The producer had the nerve to offer the page numbers.[41]

3

The issue of Harding's papers took its beginnings from the decision of the president's widow to cull her husband's papers, to do "what Warren would do," and thereby and with the best of intentions she inaugurated the confusion that was to continue for many years.[42] After Harding's funeral she returned to Washington to pack her White House belongings and in the course of the packing undertook to destroy anything that might bring criticism to her husband's memory or that of his administration.

The story of destruction of papers was nothing if not complicated. The widow undoubtedly destroyed papers, but not nearly as much as was thought. She really got hold of only one group of Harding papers, perhaps the most important group but a fairly small body of papers—and, to be sure, in the way of complex bodies of material it was not possible to obliterate traces or marks of issues on subjects, and if handled by amateurs the impossibility was simply underlined. The group of papers that Florence Harding culled was on the second floor of the White House in the president's study; ever since construction of the executive offices by Theodore Roosevelt at the time of the refurbishing that was arranged for the White House in 1902, presidents have had two offices and kept papers in both. The president's widow was assisted by her social secretary, Laura Harlan, and her husband's military aide, Major Ora M. Baldinger, the latter a protégé of the first lady because years earlier he had been one of her *Marion Star* newsboys. The group worked in the second-floor office from August 11 to August 17, and then the widow left the White House to stay for a short time, prior to her return to Marion, with her friends the McLeans and took some papers to their estate, Friendship, to read and perhaps destroy. Meanwhile Baldinger sent to Marion several—the number was between five and eight—large wooden crates of second-floor papers, crates measuring one foot wide and one foot high and ten feet in length.

The papers were packed tightly into the boxes. Upon her arrival in Marion, Mrs. Harding and Baldinger spent more time, Baldinger thought it was six weeks, going through the remaining papers and destroying individual papers or files that she felt should be eliminated, with the result that the boxes shipped from Washington were reduced from between five and eight down to two. Destruction hence was at least as high as 60 percent.

Not long after she finished with the second-floor papers the widow returned to Washington on what was to be her last trip, and while there she made another large error in regard to her husband's papers. She talked with Charles Moore, an official of the Library of Congress, and told him forthrightly that she had burned all of the papers. She must have known she had burned only part of them. Moreover, she did not know that other important groups of papers remained. She was an ill woman, which may have accounted for her remark. She said the same thing to the publisher Frank N. Doubleday, whom she also saw in Washington.

The result of her saying she had burned the papers was that, a year after her death, Moore made her remark public, doubtless with the intention of putting pressure on the Harding Memorial Association to give up the papers it had. He may have realized that other groups of papers were not yet in the hands of the association. In any event all he accomplished was to give the impression that the Harding papers, for good and sufficient reasons, had been destroyed, an impression that did no good to the memory of the late president. For years thereafter journalists and even some historians asserted that the papers were burned. Adams so wrote in 1939 and followed in the same paragraph by relating that government agents in 1922 destroyed a biography of Harding by Chancellor, the author of the 1920 pamphlet on Harding's supposed Negro blood, as if the Harding papers and the Chancellor biography were of the same importance, doubtless realizing that his account gave the impression that everything pertaining to Harding needed destruction.

In fact, as mentioned, there were other groups of Harding papers, notably the papers of the executive offices, found in the basement of the White House in 1929, where Harding's former secretary, George B. Christian Jr., perhaps inadvertently had left them. By that time Florence Harding was dead (she died in 1924), and these papers went to Marion intact, into the custody of the Harding Memorial Association in accord with the widow's will concerning the Harding papers generally.

Meanwhile officers of the association had possession of papers from the period when Harding was editor of the *Marion Star* as well as from his early days in office, which included two terms in the Ohio senate and one term as lieutenant governor. Florence Harding would have had opportunity to go through those papers, but there was no evidence she looked at them during her culling sessions with the papers from the White House's second-floor office—no evidence appeared when years later the *Star* papers opened with the other Harding papers.

The fourth and last group of papers came from Christian, who had kept them in his house in Washington before giving them to the Library of Congress, which in turn gave them to the Harding Memorial Association in 1953. These were papers on Harding's term in the U.S. Senate, together with papers for the presidential campaign of 1920.

On October 10, 1963, the transfer of papers from Marion to Columbus to the Ohio Historical Society began, and the papers—350,000 pages of them, in eight hundred archival boxes—were opened on April 25, 1964.

Compared to the odyssey of the papers, the biographer Francis Russell's discovery of the Carrie Phillips letters and their final disposition (which was closure under an arrangement with the Harding heirs) was of far less importance, though it offered a good deal more drama, and, as before, any drama connected with Harding's memory was likely to do more harm than good.

The existence of letters to the wife of James E. Phillips, owner of the Uhler-Phillips dry-goods store on East Center Street in Marion, had not been generally known prior to Russell's trip to Marion in the autumn of 1963, though the possibility of a liaison had been discussed in several books since Chancellor had written in his 1922 biography that Harding and Carrie Phillips had met on occasion at Upper Sandusky, twenty miles north of Marion. References to her in subsequent books were veiled because to have named her in a book published by a traceable publisher (Chancellor's was credited to "The Sentinal Press," a name with a gross misspelling and no place of publication) could have opened the author and publisher to court action as libelous. Nan Britton mentioned Carrie Phillips in *The President's Daughter,* albeit with a pseudonym, "a certain Mrs. Arnold." She repeated Chancellor's assertion that Republican leaders in 1920 gave "Mrs. Arnold" money to go to Japan; she did not mention precise payments, relating only that the beautiful Mrs. Arnold had taken a trip to the Orient. The source that inspired Russell's trip to Marion was *Masks in a Pageant,* which referred to "a primrose detour from Main Street which Florence Kling, the Duchess [Mrs. Harding], had chosen to ignore." Means wrote cautiously of "a milliner in Marion" whom he described as Mrs. Milliner; Jess Smith, he claimed, told him about her, and spoke of her as a presidential ex-flame, using one of his, Smith's, favorite words, *lollapalooza.* Mrs. Milliner claimed to have letters, which Means obtained for fifteen thousand dollars. Adams repeated White's primrose path description, with an embellishment, a couplet about the late president:

> His right eye was a good little eye,
> But his left eye loved to roam.[43]

Russell's course should have been taken earlier by some Harding scholar, and the fact that it was not says something about scholarly reading, that the scholars were not reading all of the literature they believed to be journalistic, even though they cited it.

Russell had only to ask in Marion if anyone remembered the name of the store about which White wrote in order to learn that it was the Uhler-Phillips establishment. Several people told him that a Marion attorney had letters from Harding to Mrs. James Phillips; upon calling on the attorney, Donald Williamson, Russell received an invitation to look at the letters. Williamson had found them in 1956 when Mrs. Phillips, a recluse who lived in a house with six dogs, was so deteriorated in health that she had to have a guardian and went to a nursing home. He had cleaned out her house preparatory to selling it, discovered a locked closet, and upon opening it found a cardboard box with ninety-eight Harding letters written between 1910 and 1920, some short, several running twenty pages, one to forty. Mrs. Phillips died in 1960.

The enterprising Russell could not have found the Phillips letters at a worse time. At that precise moment the historical society was shipping the Harding papers from Marion to Columbus. The first shipment had gone to Columbus on October 10, 1963, the second and what would prove the largest went on October 15, and Russell by chance had gone to Marion on October 19. The Phillips letters contained no secrets of state and were almost worthless in their few testimonies about public matters but did show the later president's momentary love for a woman other than his wife and for that reason would be embarrassing to the Harding family. If the family and the officers of the Harding Memorial Association learned of what Russell had found, they could stop the transfer of the remaining Harding papers to the Ohio Historical Society and perhaps tie up any use of the papers that had arrived.

What happened thereafter, like the handling of the papers by Mrs. Harding, could hardly have been worse. Anything connected with President Harding seemed to make everyone act irrationally. After Williamson showed Russell the letters, the biographer confided his discovery to the manuscript curator of the historical society, Kenneth W. Duckett. Russell and Duckett obtained the Phillips letters from the dead woman's guardian, Williamson, who had no legal right either to have kept the letters from 1956 until 1963 or to have given them away, and took them to the society in Columbus. Duckett said no more about them for several months, until April 15, 1964, when he told the society's president, Fred J. Milligan, of their existence. The latter told his board, and they advised him to talk to the Marion County probate judge, Edward J. Ruzzo, for Carrie Phillips in her last years had been penniless; the state had paid her old-age insurance, which provided the money for her to live in the nursing home. If the letters had monetary value, which they obviously did, they would have to be used to extinguish the debt of the estate.

Meanwhile, through Duckett's involvement the society had been incautious enough to allow Harding biographers working in the society's search room to see the letters, and the Harding heirs represented by the president's nephew, Dr. George T. Harding III, were understandably up in arms, both because of their embarrassment from discovery of the letters and because allowing scholars to see them was likely to mean publication, which would violate the well-known rule of common law that literary rights reside in the writer or his or her heirs, not in whoever has physical possession. If it did not mean publication, that is, quotation, it could mean paraphrasing, which would be as bad and maybe worse because it would be inexact. The Harding heirs enjoined quotation of the letters. Judge Ruzzo ordered the letters sealed and turned over to an administrator for sale.

At that juncture the Harding family members allowed their sentiments about the letters to become known, which was not wise, although again understandable—they wanted the more lurid of the letters, which contained open sexual references, destroyed, or at least desired some sort of protection of the president's memory from "printing lurid details," so their lawyer said in an interview. "My clients," he explained, "would like to destroy the letters, but I don't think that will happen. They want to suppress them."[44]

The possibility of destruction was unlikely but seemed quite real. Duckett was told "that one of the board members . . . became quite violent when he learned about these things and said something to the effect that they should be destroyed." This was not a member of the Harding family but of the historical society board, Judge Lehr Fess, son of the former Ohio senator, Simeon D. Fess. Duckett said that when he, Duckett, and the president of the board, Milligan, went to Marion and conferred with Judge Ruzzo, the judge had said, "You want a solution to your problem, send the things back up here and we will get rid of them." At that remark the former guardian of Mrs. Phillips, Williamson, added, "Yes, we will burn them," to which Milligan twice responded, "Fine." During the day in which the letters were discussed in Marion, Williamson said to Milligan, "I bet you wish, Fred, I burned those damned things when I got my hands on them the first time." Milligan did not answer. Duckett became so anxious about the Phillips letters that he told a *New York Times* reporter, "I have heard the words 'burn, destroy and suppress' so many times since I acquired the papers that I have determined that extraordinary precautions must be taken to ensure their preservation and their use by historians."[45] Before the letters passed into the hands of Judge Ruzzo, Duckett arranged for the editor of *American Heritage,* Oliver Jensen, to receive photographic copies, which Jensen deposited in the vault of a New York bank.

Gradually, and the process took seven years, from 1964 until 1971, during which time any development in the case was public because of its being a matter of court record, the strange, almost weird, business of protecting the Phillips letters wound down to an arrangement satisfactory to all parties. The suit by Dr. Harding, which asked for the impounding of the letters and one million dollars in damages, was against Duckett, Russell, the McGraw-Hill Publishing Company (Russell's publisher), and the American Heritage Publishing Company. When the *New York Times* published quotations from two or three of the letters, Dr. Harding added it to the list of defendants. He said the printing of material by the newspaper resulted in embarrassment, extreme humiliation, and mental suffering to the Harding heirs; it was all legal boilerplate but read well in the newspapers. When he added the *New York Times* to his suit Dr. Harding also added one of the Ohio Historical Society trustees and the editor of the *Dayton Journal Herald,* Glenn Thompson, because Thompson had suggested to Duckett the microfilming of the letters. The *Times's* lawyer sought to have the case tried in federal court, because ownership of both the *New York Times* and *American Heritage* was outside the State of Ohio and he probably thought a federal judge would be more sympathetic than a state judge, but a federal judge in Columbus through a technicality remanded the case to a common pleas judge. All the while Judge Ruzzo in Marion was arranging to have the letters appraised by experts selected from a list provided by the chief of the manuscript division of the Library of Congress, David C. Mearns. Guesses as to the value of the letters ranged as high as $100,000, exclusive of literary rights. The appraisers set their value at $15,000. Ruzzo stipulated payment of $3,900 to the appraisers, the administrator of the Phillips estate, and the administrator's lawyer, and $3,854.11 to the State of Ohio, the latter being the amount Mrs. Phillips cost the state for old-age insurance. The question became whether Mrs. Phillips's daughter, Isabelle Mather, of Genoa City, Wisconsin, desired to accept responsibility for the debts of the estate and take the letters in return or let the letters go up for sale at auction. She paid the debts, took the letters, and in January 1965 Dr. Harding bought them from her. In 1971 Dr. Harding's lawyer concluded an agreement with the defendants to send the microfilm copy of the letters to the Ohio Historical Society and for *American Heritage* to pay the physician $10,000, in exchange for which the Harding family would donate the letters to the Library of Congress with the proviso that they not be opened until July 29, 2014. The case against the *New York Times* was dismissed, and Dr. Harding dropped his demand for one million dollars in damages.

Considerably more than the mishandling of the Harding papers by Mrs. Harding, the affair of the Phillips letters kept the light of publicity on the memory of President Warren G. Harding. During Harding's lifetime there had been much talk of his extraordinary good luck; that everything turned out so well for him, including the way in which he rose to the presidency after a single Senate term. When the president died all this good fortune came to an end.

Carrie Phillips, one might conclude, was a schemer, not very interesting intellectually, a grade school teacher in Bucyrus who to escape her unmanageable pupils (Russell assumed) at the age of twenty-one married the thirty-year-old "Jim" Phillips. A head shorter than Carrie, Phillips was the owner of a thriving store and could get her away from Bucyrus to a larger town with more cultural advantages, among them associating with neighbors such as the Hardings. Carrie Phillips was physically attractive. If her face, as Russell appraised it, was cold and almost hard, "the lines of her body were warmly female." Duckett described her as "pleasantly chubby, a sort of Gibson girl." Her face, he agreed, was not sensual. "She certainly was no Mata Hari. But she had something that attracted men."[46] The affair began in 1905 when Jim Phillips was ill in the Battle Creek Sanitarium (which Harding had recommended to him) and Mrs. Harding, suffering an intense episode of a longtime kidney malady, was in a Columbus hospital. The romance passed through phases when Harding met her in New York while allegedly on a hunting trip to Texas. He seems to have met her in Europe before the World War when she was living in Germany. Duckett said in 1972, when the court decision on the letters allowed him to speak of their contents in general terms, that Florence Harding knew of her husband's relationship with Carrie Phillips almost from its start, probably as early as 1909 when the Hardings and Phillipses toured Europe together. The letters, he said, showed that Carrie Phillips lived in the hope that Harding would divorce his wife and marry her and that once she tried to precipitate a divorce by sending letters to Harding from another of her lovers.[47]

The *New York Times* published parts of a letter from Harding to Mrs. Phillips in 1920 that showed she was blackmailing him, as Chancellor claimed two years after the blackmail took place—raising a question of whether part of the blackmail consisted of her telling the story to her Marion neighbors. Indeed Chancellor wrote almost as much, although claiming that it happened afterward: "The Phillips [*sic*] went to Japan early in October, but not until Mrs. Phillips, who is a very talkative woman, had told all her friends just what she was to receive." The letter quoted by the *New York Times* showed that she desired a considerable sum, more than Harding could afford, and that he offered to return to Marion if she desired. If he was to remain in public service, if she thought he could be more helpful to the American people that way, he promised to pay her

$5,000 annually as long as he was in office. The letters seem to have said nothing about $25,000 and $2,000 a month, the terms Chancellor described.[48]

Discovery of the letters raised obvious questions. One was in regard to the account of Jess Smith in Daugherty's brother's bank, "Jess Smith Extra No. 3." Another was whether the undoubted affair made more likely the truth of the charges by Nan Britton. Both Russell and the *New York Times* reporter R. W. Apple answered the latter question by saying that the letters made Ms. Britton's claims more likely. But one could argue the other way. When the letters became public knowledge in the summer of 1964, Ms. Britton told a reporter for the *Chicago American,* "I did not know about Mrs. Phillips or about the letters President Harding wrote to her."[49] She may well have said more than she intended. For the first time the glass of publicity was focusing on another woman, and that might have galled her. The remark also sounded as if she was nonplussed and gave out a statement without calculating it, unlike her various press remarks of the more distant past. In that unrehearsed remark she may have been revealing what the *New York Daily News* reporter John O'Donnell published in 1927, that Richard Wightman had written *The President's Daughter.* The next year Patricia Wightman in a separation suit said the same thing. Wightman could have learned about Carrie Phillips from reading Chancellor's book. Despite the stories of its destruction (Means claimed he accomplished that task), copies survived, and even though the book was a rare item there was a copy in the New York Public Library (the Library of Congress and Ohio Historical Society also possess copies). If Wightman wrote *The President's Daughter,* he would have used the copy of the Chancellor book in the New York Public Library. He would have employed the pseudonym "Mrs. Arnold." Given the haste with which Ms. Britton's book, a long book, was written, its supposed author could have forgotten some of the things Wightman put in it, including the references to Carrie Phillips as "Mrs. Arnold." When she said in 1964 that she had not known of Mrs. Phillips, she would have been admitting that her own case was insecure, because Wightman had created it for her.[50]

One might observe about the Phillips affair and the letters that supported it, and apart from the point made earlier about what ill luck it represented in the series of misfortunes that dogged Harding's memory, that like the Teapot Dome scandal so the Phillips liaison was blown far out of proportion. It did not add to Harding's stature. By the end of the affair in 1920 he must have known that his judgment in involving himself, quite apart from the impropriety, had been terrible; he laid himself open to blackmail and for a while must have been in danger of having to withdraw from the nomination—from what the *New York Times* printed of the blackmail letter of 1920. One senses that Florence Harding stood behind him in this near-tragic blunder, for if (as Duckett said) she knew about the affair she must also have known—Harding would have told her, for it involved a large sum—what he was up against. If indeed she supported him, which one can guess was the case, her standing up for him gives her memory an almost noble quality, as compared to the calumnies it suffered in the years after her death. And, finally, measuring the episode, historians need to place it against other such happenings to American public figures throughout the country's history, large figures such as Benjamin Franklin, Alexander Hamilton, and within Harding's time Grover Cleveland. The president of 1885–1889 and 1893–1897 admitted a connection with a Buffalo woman, Maria Halpin, who like Carrie Phillips had connections with other men. He took responsibility for her son even though he was not certain he was the father. This scrape came out just before Cleveland's election to the presidency in 1884 and thereafter was never held against him personally nor against his administration.

4

At last, in 1964, the papers became available, and Harding enthusiasts (what few there were of them) and Harding haters alike had opportunity to hold up their hero or villain against his own papers and a dozen and more collections of Harding's associates, also available at the Ohio Historical Society, and see what the truth was about the man from Marion. The resultant biographies were, by and large, disappointing.

First to publish was a scholar from Cambridge University, Andrew Sinclair, whose biography *The Available Man: The Life behind the Masks of Warren Gamaliel Harding* appeared in 1965, a year after the papers opened. Considering the size of the papers and the usual lead time for publication of books—at least half a year between turning in manuscript and receiving finished, bound volumes—a reader might have wondered whether

Sinclair was quick with his book, and the answer has to be that he was. The book did not show enough of the new material; it used the papers lightly.[51]

Sinclair chose as his theme not the idea of Harding's availability, which in American politics means that a man or woman has not antagonized any major group of possible supporters, but a notion of there having been various "myths" in the American mind around the year 1920, myths that Harding perpetuated at a time when there should have been a large moment of truth. The notion of myths was a contrivance, perhaps designed to take the author across the thin ice of his research in the Harding papers. The author's principal myth was that Harding represented the generality of Americans when in the census of 1920 it became apparent for the first time that rural—that is, small-town and country—America had given way to urban America. Sinclair said Harding thereby was behind the times, which may have been true in the sense that he had been brought up in the country and in small towns, which was hardly his fault, but he might have been able (Sinclair obviously did not think so) to understand cities despite his residential handicap. Having pointed out Harding's unfortunate accident of birth and upbringing, the author evoked other myths that mostly seem unmythical: he wrote of the myth of the Country Boy (which was true), of the Self-made Man (no man or woman is self-made), of the Presidential State (by which he meant that the president constituted the government, another theory seldom believed), of the Political Innocent (here was no myth, for no one saw Harding as politically innocent), of the Guardian Senate (this myth had its believers), of America First (which also had some believers). He wrote of the myths of the Reluctant Candidate, Dark Horse, Smoke-filled Room, Solemn Referendum (that was President Wilson's myth in 1920), and Best Minds. In his biography of Harding the citation of myths became, after a while, annoying.

The book's principal fault was the author's refusal to believe that ability at politics is a mark of intelligence. The author was sure Harding "remained the small-town gentleman playing a part too large for him." The president had a "fuzzy mentality." He was "a man of mediocre intellect." His predecessor Wilson described people like Harding as possessing bungalow minds. Harding, Sinclair wrote, "knew nothing of the science of government." Withal he admitted that Harding was no "political innocent" and fought with "the craftiest politicians of his day." Harding was a "hardworking and shrewd Ohio politician. He was always his own master. He used compromise and humility as political tactics . . . he was a formidable opponent in an election."[52] Shades of H. S. Truman! The latter political leader, now much appreciated, always considered political judgment as much a part of intellect as the thoughts of anyone in any other walk of life, such as a physician, clergyman, or scholar.

The book had a few problems with understanding the American scene, doubtless because of Sinclair's British background. The author placed in Ohio the Battle Creek Sanitarium where Harding and Jim Phillips went on occasion (this lapse also said something about Sinclair's editors at Macmillan). As for American colleges and universities, the author misunderstood the nature of Ohio Central College in Iberia, from which Harding graduated. He said the college's curriculum was insufficient. Of course it was insufficient. Ohio Central was naught but a high school or what in the nineteenth century was known as an academy; Harding attended it for two years and graduated at the age of seventeen. American colleges and universities of size and quality were hardly visible until the 1890s, when a baby boom after the Civil War and the training of faculty members in German universities at last brought the twin requisites of enrollment and scholarship.

Other details were out of order. On the train moving cross-country to Tacoma in 1923 the author placed Secretary Hoover, who joined the Harding party on the West Coast. He exaggerated the casualties in the Veterans' Bureau scandal, two suicides he wrote, when there was one suicide. He put the oilman Doheny in jail, though the oilman never went to jail. He placed the death of Florence Harding "within six months" of that of Dr. Sawyer, which was technically true but disconcertingly general, as she died two months later. He discovered 250 Harding letters to Carrie Phillips, which number he found in the *New York Times* rather than reading the ninety-eight letters in Columbus, and he also declared that *American Heritage* bought the letters from Mrs. Phillips's estate.[53]

It is perhaps unfair to relate these smaller errors, but in regard to the fight between President Wilson and the Senate concerning the League of Nations and the Treaty of Versailles at the end of Wilson's administration—which was the prelude to Harding's electoral victory in 1920, a matter Sinclair might have studied in detail—Sinclair remarked flatly that President Wilson "lay in a coma in the White House from the fall of

1919 to the spring of 1920," which was a new interpretation of the Wilson era, since the ill president was never in a coma. In relating a prime event in foreign affairs of the Harding administration, Harding's endorsement of United States membership in the World Court during the transcontinental train trip to Tacoma, he confused the World Court, composed of League of Nations–appointed jurists, with what he described as "The Hague Court," which was a panel of judges chosen by signatories of a protocol produced by the First Hague Peace Conference of 1899, from which governments of nations might, if they wished, draw for arbitration of their differences.[54]

Sinclair accepted every word in *The President's Daughter,* with a sniff to anyone who disagreed: "In this work, Miss Britton proved to all except the most charitable that she was the mother of Harding's daughter."[55]

In 1968, three years after Sinclair's publication, Russell's book came out and was a best seller, offering misinformation of a different sort. Earlier, in an *American Heritage* article, Russell had discerned four "mysteries" about Harding, and he set them out in his biography. One was the color of Harding's skin; the president's face was dark-hued, and Russell bolstered Chancellor's accusation that Harding possessed Negro blood. From this contemporary canard (people in the race-ridden 1920s considered it an accusation) came the title *The Shadow of Blooming Grove: Warren G. Harding and His Times.* The second mystery, "no less disturbing," was the "woman question." The third was the manner of the president's death; the fourth was the fate of his private papers.[56]

Of Russell's mysteries, none was enigmatic. They were no more worth reading about than Sinclair's myths, as Russell in his 663 pages—twice as many as Sinclair's book—gradually revealed. The mystery of the woman question he handled in part by leaving cryptic gaps on his pages when he long since had known—the issue had arisen four years before—that he could not safely quote from the Phillips letters. For the rest of it he entertained readers with descriptions from Nan Britton's book. Like Sinclair, although with far more elaboration, he accepted anything Ms. Britton wrote. There was no question about it. He allowed that if this affair "could not be documented to the satisfaction of Dr. George Harding," the "gushing, redundant" pages of her book rang true. It was impossible, he said, rather queerly, to counterfeit such artlessness.[57]

In addition to retailing sex, Russell wrote in an attractive way, as when he described Harding on the Chautauqua circuit. To read the account was to believe it:

> After the applause, the stir, and the clatter of wooden seats, the audience filed out into the cool air of the summer evening. No one was very sure of just what the speaker had said, but everyone going home under the stars remembered how well he had said it! Harding enjoyed such folksy audiences, enjoyed them even more when the Duchess's health kept her in Marion. Doggedly she traveled with him whenever she could manage it, perched by his side in the daycoach from one Chautauqua center to the next, her edged voice rasping at him all the way, querulous, persistent, while he sulked in his plush seat, a cigar wedged into his mouth, his frown growing deeper under her nagging until finally he would turn on her with "goddammit, shut up!" and she would lapse into brief, offended silence.[58]

Francis Russell was a talented essayist and writer who, when dealing with what he knew, was impressive. Born in Boston in 1910, he had grown up with memories of the Boston police strike of 1919; one of his school friends was the son of a striking policeman who had been dismissed by the police commissioner, under direction of Governor Coolidge. He remembered how proud Officer Fitzgibbons had been of his uniform and how after the strike one of the policeman's children was playing with his father's helmet and a spoon, sitting on the curb in front of the Fitzgibbonses' house. He wrote an interesting if large-D Democratic account of the strike, flamboyantly entitled *A City in Terror*. He wrote about Sacco and Vanzetti and arranged to have the bullets that were fired at the paymaster, who was killed, analyzed ballistically against the murder weapon, which had never been done; he discovered, and published, the fact that at least one of the two men electrocuted in 1927 was guilty. But when he turned to the biography of Harding, for which he was awarded two Guggenheim fellowships, the result was not a scholarly success.

The Randolph C. Downes biography published in 1970, *The Rise of Warren Gamaliel Harding, 1865–1920*, neither subtracted from nor added to Harding's stature and received little attention in the group of biographies published after the opening of the papers. It amounted to a close, detailed, and—because of the byzantine nature of Ohio politics at the turn of the twentieth century—almost impossible to remember narrative of Harding's political career prior to the presidency. Downes knew a great deal about Harding. For years he devoted his life to Harding. A friend and colleague at the University of Toledo, Robert Freeman Smith, reported to the present writer that when the Harding papers were opened at the Ohio Historical Society, Downes worked so hard he could not finish his labors during the hours allotted to researchers and was accustomed to elude the society's building guards and secrete himself in the stacks at night, where he could read the documents in the small hours. Kenneth Duckett disputes this possibility but admits that one morning the guards did find Downes asleep in a society office.

In one respect other than its details, and its ending in 1920, Downes's book may have disappointed readers, considering the juicy descriptions Sinclair and especially Russell presented of Nan Britton and Carrie Phillips. The book contained nothing on either of these individuals, which was perhaps a relief, but nonetheless curious. The reason must have been that when he submitted his manuscript to the Ohio State University Press the director, Weldon A. Kefauver, sent it to Dr. Harding. The Harding descendant had heard Downes speak at a meeting of the Harding Memorial Association and listened to the historian air his feelings about his inability to see the Phillips letters. Furious that Downes chose a celebration in Marion to make this complaint, Dr. Harding was ready to look over the manuscript with care and did so, informing Kefauver, who informed Downes, that certain references should come out.

There is not much point in going into the issue that arose between Downes, on the one side, and Dr. Harding and Kefauver on the other. The Harding heir and Kefauver received a considerable criticism. It certainly could be argued that scholarship does not need censorship. Still, it was not necessary for Harding biographers to make as much of the woman question as Sinclair and Russell did. Downes, too, had put himself in a corner on the Britton matter. It was wrong of him to support Ms. Britton's allegations—he should have supported President Harding's reputation until he discovered reason not to. When Dr. Harding asked Kefauver to remove the offending passages in Downes's manuscript, he was only making a request and could not have forced the issue. Kefauver on his part felt that there had been too many arguments about Harding and may be excused for tiring of them. Downes had another volume to go and could make his points there.[59]

Turning backward, chronologically speaking, to Robert K. Murray's book, published in 1969, the sole biography of quality to emerge after the opening of the papers, it is necessary to look only at this remarkable author's explanation of why American historians failed to understand Harding. Murray offered advice beyond his description of the journalists, drawing them as Rooseveltians or Wilsonians. In his last pages he made interesting speculations about the training of historians after World Wars I and II. He wrote that as the politics of the journalists affected their conclusions, so did the training of the historians.

Historians are not a fascinating group, no large subject for speculation, except that they write the books and make the historical speculations, and now that the Harding era is too far back for the journalists to distort it, it is of interest why the historians picked up the journalists' ideas. The reason may well be, as the biographer related, that the historians who taught the biographers and other historical writers of the 1960s not only grew up with such descriptions of presidential administrations as those offered by Gilbert in the *Mirrors* books but also enjoyed the essays of Mencken and read the journalism of White, Allen, Nevins, Longworth, Sullivan, and Adams.

But something more was at fault in the judgments of historians about the Harding era. Why, despite the passage of half a century and more since 1945, do historians continue to place Harding at the bottom of the lists they make of presidents? Arthur M. Schlesinger Sr. polled experts on the presidency, mostly historians, in 1948 and 1962, and Harding came in last. Those ratings were before the Harding papers opened. In 1981 a historian at William Penn College, David I. Porter, asked forty-one colleagues to rate the presidents; the next year Steve Neal of the *Chicago Tribune* conducted a poll; and that same year the Harding biographer, Murray, together with Tim H. Blessing did an extensive and unlike the others statistically sophisticated poll. The sixth and seventh polls in 1995 were by William J. Ridings and Stuart B. McIver in *Presidential Studies Quarterly* and again by Neal, this time in the *Chicago Sun-Times*.[60] In every poll Harding came in last. It is true that the historians who rated the presidents in the two Schlesinger polls would not have read Murray's biography.

But all the later historians could have read it, and would that not have raised Harding at least above Ulysses S. Grant, Richard M. Nixon, James Buchanan, and Andrew Johnson?

The answer may be that because of pressure to publish so as to receive stature in their profession—publish or perish—and if not that then to produce lectures that engage students, the historians saved themselves the trouble of reading more than they had to. They went to the books of the journalists rather than those of the historians or, if the latter, then read Russell, from whom they could learn what Harding said to his wife while riding the day coach on the Chautauqua circuit, or about Nan Britton and Carrie Phillips.

Four

CALVIN COOLIDGE, THE MAN
AND THE PRESIDENT

T HE MAN was president of the United States, and for many years people have asked how such a man, a Dickensian character, could be president, how he became so attractive to the American people that they would have given him another term in 1928 if he had asked for it. Perhaps the fault lay with the Boston department store owner Frank W. Stearns, who sponsored Coolidge politically. Stearns it was who first talked his Amherst College friends into advancing Coolidge against the Harvard politicians who were dominating Massachusetts. In 1919 just after the Boston police strike and Governor Coolidge's pronouncement to Samuel Gompers about there being no right to strike against the public safety, Stearns raised his sights to the presidency; he sponsored a collection of Coolidge speeches entitled *Have Faith in Massachusetts,* bought sixty-five thousand copies from Houghton Mifflin, and gave them to anyone who could read. He said that Calvin Coolidge was as great as Abraham Lincoln. All this for what the Boston Brahmin and Harvard professor Barrett Wendell described as a "small, hatched-faced, colorless man, with a tight-shut, thin-lipped mouth, very chary of words."[1] This for a man who after marrying the most attractive girl in Northampton could be as offhand with her and their sons as he was with his constituents.

There also was a question of how this man could carry on the duties of president of the United States in an era such as the golden twenties. Coolidge's entire personality stood against it. Alfred P. Dennis, who knew him from the turn of the century when Dennis was a history teacher at Smith College and the two ate at a boardinghouse, claimed Coolidge belonged to the eighteenth century and only found himself in the age of mobility—"light, heat and power distributed in an instant over copper wires, intelligence flashed across continents, under oceans and through the air in the twinkling of an eye, myriads of motor-cars darting to and fro on our public highways, a world on wheels, restless, avid, resistlessly pushing and struggling onward; fortunes made or lost in a day, big fees, high stakes."[2]

1

The Coolidge personality, let us face it, was not easy; suffice it to say that some of it was shyness, some of it was out of rural Vermont, and some derived from the pressures of high office. Some of it was attractive in a Plymouth Notch way, and this was what the American people saw and liked. Some of it was quite unattractive, and for the most part they did not see it and hence could not know whether they liked it or not.

The shyness was undeniable. Judge Henry P. Field of Northampton, in whose office Coolidge studied law, said again and again, "Calvin is shy." It often was remarked what Coolidge himself said, that when he was a child and people were in the kitchen of the house at Plymouth Notch he hated to go through the old kitchen door. "Every time I meet a stranger, I've got to go through the old kitchen door, back home, and that's not easy."[3] When he was president, he liked to have people around whom he had known. The assistant White House physician, Dr. Boone, a lieutenant commander in the U.S. Navy, found that by navy custom his tour of duty in the White House would be coming to an end, and spoke to the president about it, mentioning the possibility of serving with the marines in China. Coolidge listened, then took the cigar out of his mouth and said, speaking in his New England twang, that "it was very difficult for him to become acquainted with people, that he didn't warm up to people readily, and it took him quite a long time before he felt on a very familiar basis. He said I had been there ever since he became president."[4]

Then there was rural Vermont, which surely accounted for his laconic nature. In Vermont the winters were cold, and the hot weather in summers was short-lived. Springs and autumns were diminished by cold nights. The climate did not lend itself to unmeasured conversation. Nor did the Vermont soil give encouragement. Just to stay alive, people had to work hard. Before the work, they prepared for it, girding themselves, and afterward they were tired. It was a straitened place. Luxury and leisure were not at hand. Coolidge's youth was only a century removed from the time of settlement, which was mostly after the Revolutionary War. Agriculture had just gotten started when the Erie Canal opened up the competition for western lands, and fields everywhere in New England passed back into wilderness, with only the stone walls of earlier times reminding visitors of what had been.

The laconic nature of the man was well known. He showed it even with his father. Boone one time was aboard the *Mayflower* and watched the president talking with his father, Colonel John Coolidge. As the beautiful ship built in the 1890s was cruising along—the ship that Coolidge's successor, Herbert Hoover, decommissioned as his first act of presidential economy—Boone saw Coolidge sitting on one end of a davenport with his father on the other, with quite a space between them. They were looking out along the Potomac as the scenery was passing, not saying a word. As Boone stood there, the president in his nasal voice and without looking at his father, spoke out straight across the waters, "How is the sheep business?" Sheep were the only product of rural New England that made a profit.

Without turning his head toward his son, looking straight ahead, Colonel Coolidge said, "Good."

Another long pause, and the president inquired, "What are they bringing the pound?"

After a sizable silence his father replied with the price he was getting.[5]

The president's measured remarks baffled his friends and political associates, who needed to find out what was on the presidential mind. Stearns told Mark Sullivan that all the conversation he ever had with Coolidge would not make two days of the talk of ordinary men who were friends. Senator William M. Butler, who had been the Boston representative of the late Murray Crane, the Republican leader in Massachusetts, and had known Coolidge for many years, told Boone he often did not know how to take Coolidge because the president said so little. "He leaves one in suspense and in an indefinite state of mind, not knowing how to deduce from what the president tells one."[6] Butler was managing Coolidge's 1924 campaign, and at that moment Secretary of the Navy Curtis D. Wilbur had made a bad speech out West, and Butler was wishing the president would find a way to return Wilbur permanently to California, his home state, but did not know how to get the president to do it. Secretary of Commerce Hoover in 1927–1928 and later as president found himself exquisitely unable to get information out of Coolidge, at the outset concerning Hoover's presidential ambitions, later about support for reelection in 1932. None of these individuals, confronting the president, wanted to talk about the sheep business, and that may have been the problem. But in the cases of Stearns and Butler, they were only seeking to advance Coolidge's purposes and needed to know them. Even Hoover was entitled to guidance.

Sometimes the president did not say anything at all. Everyone knows Stearns's tale of when Coolidge spent his first day in the White House executive offices, after President Harding passed on, and the president called five times for Stearns. Each time the latter went into the presidential office, circled around, said nothing to Coolidge, who said nothing to him. Even for Stearns, who had seen a great deal of Coolidge, this was unnerving. "A dog would have done equally well," he said.[7] A state department official and Harvard graduate who was perhaps too thoughtful about the problem wrote the American ambassador in London that the president "listens to what one has to say and makes no comment. But if the ideas expressed appeal to him he acts on them weeks or months later. They are always stored in his mind, to be used when the opportunity occurs."[8]

From the tightness of Vermont, one can guess, came another quality other than brevity or silences, not usually noticed by outsiders but apparent within the Coolidge family circle. This was a steely unwillingness to unbend, which took the form of refusing to do what would have made life easier for everyone around him. Relations within the family, one would have thought, might not have possessed this quality. Yet such was the case. When he courted Grace Goodhue in Northampton he was strangely reticent. He should have been on his best behavior with Grace's friends but instead almost frightened them. The stories of how he acted are well known and for the most part true, as Grace herself told most of them. She was such an opposite from him. In any sort of ordinary relationship, and perhaps simply from being around her, he should have unbent and become more like her—become, in a word, livable. She was such a good catch, as his boardinghouse friend Dennis observed: "I remember Grace Goodhue vividly, hardly out of her teens when she came to Northampton.... A creature of spirit, fire, and dew, given to blithe spontaneous laughter, with eager birdlike movements, as natural and unaffected as sunlight or the sea, a soul that renders the common air sweet."[9] It may be that during the courtship when the two were by themselves Coolidge relaxed, but as soon as someone came within their presence he was stiff as a board. To use the Northampton description for him, he was a "stick."

Coolidge's refusal to unbend was striking. As he did not make any effort to get along with Grace's friends during what he must have realized was the important business of his courtship, neither did he try to make up to her mother, Mrs. Goodhue. She undoubtedly was difficult. Grace told Dr. Boone that her mother had been a selfish person and did not want the marriage. He interjected that her mother had given her to the world. Mrs. Coolidge responded that she felt that this fact, if it was a fact, had never impressed her mother. Mrs. Goodhue did not really care for her daughter's husband nor for that matter for the boys, John and Calvin Jr. Coolidge thought that Mrs. Goodhue's later popularity in the newspapers was due to his own success and perhaps concluded that she might be grateful. But both during the courtship and afterward he refused to give an inch to his mother-in-law. He would not cater to her. In visits to Northampton he never wanted to stay long with her; two days were long enough, even though his wife sensed that a little longer might help.

He was no more careful with his wife than he was with her mother. William R. Castle Jr. of the state department noticed how he walked ahead of his wife at White House musicals, observing to his diary, "I wonder whether he will continue to walk ahead of her when they leave the White House."[10] There were many other such lapses. He had a mischievous streak and when aboard the *Mayflower* may have refused to give his wife the guest list for this reason. It was very irritating to her, and if the purpose was mischief he carried it much too far. She would step into a cabin and ask Boone who was on the list. Then she would go out and greet the guests.

The president did not want his wife to have anything to do with politics and pushed the point to ridiculous lengths. He was adamant on the subject, and it was not wise for her to speak about political issues in his presence. In this respect she carefully watched the boundary he established.

On one occasion two prominent women of one of the largest and most populous states in the country came by appointment to call and confer with her, and she saw them in the Red Room. When she joined the president for lunch, she told him of the call. He asked what they wanted, and she said it was a political interest. With quite a little irritation he snapped, "Did you tell them you didn't know anything about politics?" Mrs. Coolidge replied quickly, "They found that out in one minute, if not in two minutes."[11] It is of course well known that while vacationing in the Black Hills in 1927, Coolidge drove off one morning to his temporary office in a local high school some distance away, where he summoned reporters and gave them typed-out slips announcing he would not run for the presidency the next year. Mrs. Coolidge knew nothing of the imminence of the event and only discovered what happened when her husband brought Senator Arthur Capper home to lunch and Capper told her.

Another example of Coolidge's stiffness within the family was the way in which he treated his sons. He told them what to wear. The boys brought home suits and other items they liked, and the decision was up to the head of the family. The boys left the clothes laid out, suits on the bed, hats on the dresser, until he came over from the executive offices for lunch. He had the boys try on the suits, did not ask what ones they liked, pointed his finger at one and said, "You will take that one, John," and at another, "Calvin, you will take that one." He would give the same instruction for the hats, after which he would turn quickly and leave the room.[12] He insisted that the boys wear suspenders rather than belts. He made them eat dinner in tuxedos. The latter requirement, the formality, was an expression of his respect for the presidency and the White House, but the rest of it, about the choice of clothes, had nothing to do with such matters.

There was a gulf between what Coolidge considered proper behavior and what the boys and his wife desired. Admittedly they lived in a goldfish bowl and had to be careful. When John was at Amherst he received a presidential letter advising him to go to church—John had visited somewhere, perhaps seeing his "girl," Florence Trumbull, daughter of the governor of Connecticut, and had chosen (it is difficult to believe that Florence, whom he married, would have permitted this) to go to a nightclub on a Saturday night and sleep in the next morning. The activity, and inactivity, was in the newspapers, and the president did not like it. When the *Mayflower* was in New England waters in 1925, Mrs. Coolidge would have liked to entertain young people with music and dancing. She wanted to propose it, but the president would have said, "What for? To spoil them?" She and John told Boone this when they were at Swampscott that summer.[13]

In the summer of 1926, Mrs. Coolidge did not desire to go to the Adirondacks; the president not only decided to go but refused to tell her when the departure would take place. Once there, he paid little attention to her. She wanted to have John there, as Calvin Jr. had died two years before, and the anniversary was coming up. Her husband made no promises. At last, in mid-August, John arrived, and Boone saw a gleam in Mrs. Coolidge's eyes as she gently watched her son.

Then there was the Coolidge temper, for the most part kept under wraps from anyone outside the family. It evidently came from his inability to express himself, which kept everything inward until an explosion, and from the mounting pressures on his time as he rose ever higher in his political offices. The truth was that whether in Northampton, Boston, or Washington, he was so busy pursuing his political responsibilities that he had little time. In Northampton the officeholding engrossed his days. In Boston he stayed in a slovenly hotel known as the Adams House where he cooped himself up in a single room with an air shaft. He was home on weekends for a day, but so tired and irritable that he was hardly fit to live with. Calvin Jr. was young at that time, and the boy's feelings did not turn into defiance, but in the case of John relations were awkward. Coolidge's wife was relieved when he returned to Boston.

In the presidency Coolidge usually managed to shield his anger from outsiders. When he was irritable, his assistants stayed away from him, and that helped. Once he tangled with an assistant who stood up to him, and he backed down. C. Bascom Slemp, a former Virginia congressman and a millionaire accustomed to careful treatment, who was his first presidential secretary, said that on one occasion Coolidge spoke brusquely to him, whereupon Slemp turned to the president and told him that no man heretofore had spoken to him that way and it must not happen again. Coolidge said he was sorry, that he had smoked too much the day before and Slemp should not pay attention, that he knew he was "hard to get along with."[14]

The James Haley incident in the Black Hills almost brought his temper into public notice. During that summer the secret service agent assigned to Mrs. Coolidge went out with her on a walk and got lost, and the two returned an hour or two late. Haley already had seen the president ignoring his wife. One time, he told Boone, Mrs. Coolidge caught a fishhook in her finger, and the president looked at it and walked off. She had resorted to companionship and conversation and laughter with Haley. Doubtless Coolidge saw this and did not like it. Haley told Boone that when he returned from the walk the president had "blown up."[15] Coolidge sent Haley back to Washington. The affair got into the newspapers, although not in its full detail.

The family saw a good deal more temper than did Slemp and Haley. One time during the White House years Mrs. Coolidge decided she would take up horseback riding and bought a riding habit and showed it to her husband. He was furious and shouted in anger, telling her to take it off and never let him see it again. Mrs. Coolidge related a toned-down version of this to guests aboard the *Mayflower,* but it was a good deal worse than she described.

Some of the outbursts arose during the writing of speeches. Coolidge wrote his speeches, unlike Harding, who was the first but by no means the last of the presidents to use a speechwriter (Harding often resorted to Judson C. Welliver, for whom is named the Judson Welliver Society, a group of former and present speechwriters who hold annual meetings in the nation's capital). Coolidge did not write speeches easily. "I always knew that there was some water in my well," he told Sullivan, "but that I had to pump to get it. It is not a gushing fountain."[16] It may have been trouble over the State of the Union address of 1923 that disturbed relations between Coolidge and Slemp. It was an important speech, as it set out Coolidge's campaign platform for election in 1924. The president already was troubled by Senate hearings over the Veterans' Bureau, the first of the so-called Harding scandals to emerge after his predecessor's death, and he may have heard rumbles of the Teapot Dome affair, which blew up a few days after the speech; he had a great deal on his mind.

Mrs. Coolidge told Boone that she had found it was wise not to bother him or even be close to him when he was writing a speech. "I let him alone as much as possible." After the speech was ready, his nervous system seemed to level off.[17]

Grace Coolidge once explained the presidential temper to her physician. Because Coolidge's mother had died when he was twelve, his grandmother had raised him, and he did not control his disposition as he should at all times. When he was merely tart, not furious, Grace Coolidge handled him by poking fun at him. One time the president thought he was being humorous with his naval aide, Captain Adolphus Andrews. He inquired if "public services" were being held aboard the *Mayflower* and wondered if it would not be better to hold "revival services," to which Mrs. Coolidge observed to her husband, "Yes, if you will attend, they will do you good."[18] The president had been tart that morning. But when he was under strain, concentrating, and likely to lose his temper, humor was unsuitable. On such occasions she considered herself his "safety valve." She took the force that he might expend on others. Early in their married life she had learned that if he came home from his office amiable and affable, he might have exploded that day to some caller. If he came home irritable and nervous and blew off, she consoled herself because she knew he had not done it to visitors or people in the office. Not long after they were married, she said, she knew she had to make a decision whether she could tolerate this kind of disposition, whether she loved him so much as to allow it.[19]

The president's public personality, beneath and behind the confusions, was nonetheless attractive. The White House under Grace and Calvin Coolidge was a pleasant place, where dinners and receptions were graciously handled. They were overflowing with food. The Coolidges had more houseguests than had been invited during any presidential administration up to that time. Apart from relatives, friends, and officials, Coolidge had 102 houseguests in five years and seven months, compared to Taft, who had 32 in four years; Wilson, who had 12 in eight years; and Harding, who, because of his wife's frequent illness with kidney disease, had only 5. People felt at home—even Alice Roosevelt Longworth when she learned that at long last she was pregnant rushed to the White House, asked the usher, Irwin H. (Ike) Hoover, where Grace Coolidge was, and ran up the stairs calling, "Grace, Grace, I'm going to have a baby!"[20] The president's secret service agent and walking companion, Colonel Edmund W. Starling, came to see that the president's outward reticence and aloofness (Starling did not mention the temper) were only a protective shell, that he was very shy. In his way he was a sentimental man, embarrassed about showing it. He loved his wife deeply, if in his own way. And she did him. When he died in January 1933, one wintry New England morning, and Starling learned of it, he dropped everything and took the first train for Northampton. Upon his arrival Grace Coolidge heard his voice and came hastily downstairs. He took her in his arms, and she broke into tears.

2

When Coolidge became president after the presidency of Harding, who during his lifetime was so popular, not a few political leaders believed that Harding's successor could not handle the job. One of the western senators, Peter Norbeck of South Dakota, made light of his qualities, charging that he could "no more run this big machine at Washington than could a paralytic."[21] Norbeck had seen the way in which Coolidge as vice president had painted himself into a corner, becoming so inconspicuous he was invisible. Perhaps he remembered the story about a fire at the New Willard Hotel, where Vice President and Mrs. Coolidge maintained a modest apartment and the guests considered them no more important, coming from Northampton, than their predecessors, Vice President and Mrs. Thomas R. Marshall, who had resided at North Manchester, Indiana. According to the story, when the fire was announced the hotel's guests came down into the lobby in various states of undress. When, at last, word was passed that the fire was out, Coolidge started upstairs, but the fire marshal halted him. "Who are you?" asked that functionary.

"I'm the vice president," Coolidge replied.

"All right—go ahead," said the marshal.

He went a step or two, only to be halted a second time. "What are you vice president of?" the marshal inquired suspiciously.

"I'm the vice president of the United States."

"Come right down," said the marshal. "I thought you were the vice president of the hotel."[22]

Norbeck thought him no man to head the government. "What we need," he opined, "is a regular Teddy Roosevelt house cleaning." He thought Senator Hiram Johnson of California could do the job; Johnson's record in his home state proved that. He described Coolidge as lacking "initiative and punch." The new president admittedly was judicial, "almost as judicial as Bill Taft." If Coolidge had any place in Washington it was on the Supreme Court.[23]

But then people who were close to the new center of power in Washington, the new president, changed their minds, for Coolidge's administrative abilities became evident. Secretary of Commerce Hoover and his reporter friend Sullivan at first agreed with Norbeck's appraisal. Sullivan described Coolidge to Hoover as a man who became an office boy and then went on step by step. Hoover said, "Not a man to start a new corporation."[24] Soon Hoover told Sullivan that Coolidge was a better administrator than his predecessor. "When you tell a thing to Coolidge he listens, takes it all in, and understands it promptly." Harding, he said, never cared for details. He trusted a cabinet member and took that individual's judgment. He would say, in jocular fashion, "What do you want today?" A little later another cabinet member would come in and have the same experience. Then the two things might conflict. Hoover said that would never happen with Coolidge.[25]

Coolidge's primeval point of administration, as he announced it in his *Autobiography,* consisted of "never doing anything that someone else can do for you."[26] It may have appeared as inaction, but it could well be, as Coolidge knew, far more effective than Hoover's administrative procedure, which was to have everything coming toward himself. Grace Coolidge, incidentally, was thoroughly aware of her husband's point of administration, and one time unthinkingly took it out on their son John. The time was the summer of 1926 when her husband insisted on going to the Adirondacks. At last John had come. He was playing tennis, and a secret service man was picking up the balls. John's mother told her son that he was just like his father.

The rule had a large part in the Coolidge foreign policy, which consisted mostly of envoys chasing balls in imperial regions. "If there is a troublesome situation in Nicaragua, a General [Frank R.] McCoy can manage it," wrote the president in his *Autobiography.* McCoy was a talented administrator. "If we have differences with Mexico, a Morrow can compose them." The president's onetime boardinghouse friend at Amherst College, Dwight W. Morrow, a partner of J. P. Morgan, was a skilled negotiator. So was the New York lawyer Henry L. Stimson. "If there is unrest in the Philippines, a Stimson can quiet them."[27]

Domestically, in management of his cabinet, which included that corporation head, Hoover, Coolidge practiced his rule with a vengeance. According to Starling, who either was present or learned of it from his walking companion, one of Coolidge's secretaries, Edward T. Clark, came in the office and asked if he could show the president a file of papers that Secretary of Labor James J. Davis wanted him to read. "He would like to know whether you agree with his decision," Clark said. The president's response was "I am not going to read them. You tell ol' man Davis I hired him as secretary of labor and if he can't do the job I'll get a new secretary of labor."[28] The president one day told his press conference that "the way I transact the cabinet business is to leave the head of each department the conduct of his own business." In the cabinet he did take up matters that required opinions of the members. He did not consider that one member had any business advising another member. There were exceptions, and he may have been thinking of Hoover, who always wanted to run two or three departments. Coolidge knew his rule had exceptions. He so advised the attendees at his press conference: "What I am telling you is a general principle."[29]

What a difference there was between Coolidge's administrative procedure and those of other presidents of his time. In this regard his Northampton friend Dennis described matters well, and may have heard some of the description from the president:

> Mr. [Theodore] Roosevelt, whose restless genius kept him in a ferment of activity, would have taken the first train South when the Mississippi River broke its bounds. Mr. Wilson, a more intellectual man than Mr. Coolidge, embarked on an overseas expedition for the purpose of setting aright the affairs of the Old World. It is safe to say that Mr. Coolidge in like circumstances would not have budged from the White House. As to the Mississippi floods, he served the country better by remaining at home and deputizing Mr. Hoover, who specializes in floods and famines.[30]

With Congress, the president's *Autobiography* related a similar modus operandi: "About a dozen able, courageous, reliable and experienced men in the House and the Senate can reduce the problem of legislation almost to a vanishing point."[31] The remark was less believable than the cabinet explanation, for Congress during the 1920s was almost unmanageable. Its emotional state was symbolized by the middle name of the junior senator from Iowa, Smith Wildman Brookhart. President Wilson had discovered that fact, and so had Harding; although, having been a senator, Harding understood the congressional psyche and near the end of his life was beginning to get it in order. Coolidge, unfortunately, failed in this regard. He may have given up, in belief that nothing was to be done. He seems also to have had the quaint idea that all he needed to do was communicate his hopes and preferences and await Congress's pleasure.

In attempting to manage Congress, Coolidge instituted his well-known breakfasts, which bewildered most of the people who attended them. The food was excellent; it could not have been improved upon. There was a full-service menu, including griddle cakes served with real Vermont maple syrup. The problem lay not in the food but in the purpose of the drill, which— like the president to many of his auditors—was inscrutable. There seemed no order of business, nothing beyond the free breakfast. Ike Hoover, who disliked Coolidge because the president refused to raise his salary (Hoover thought it was because Coolidge wanted to save the money and take it back to Northampton), claimed the invitees did everything possible to stay away. Senator Key Pittman of Nevada telephoned his excuse to Mrs. Pittman, who said a wheel had come off their car down the road. Senator Frederick Hale of Maine pleaded that his man had forgotten to call him. Senator Johnson averred that his barn had burned down (Hoover to the contrary, this was true; Johnson had rented a house with a barn, and the latter burned). One congressman, to Hoover's amusement, had been out all night and could not be found.[32]

Relying on the cabinet, less so on Congress, Coolidge sought to use the newspaper press to support his administration, and in this regard, in his press conferences, he did well, setting a standard against which his predecessors appeared poorly and successors until Truman did only modestly well. In Coolidge's day press conference attendance was small, no more than a dozen reporters. Old-timers like Sullivan attended occasionally but seem to have felt attendance harmed their dignity. A Harvard man, Sullivan complained to his diary about what he considered Coolidge's overconfidence, this at the beginning of the administration. In the metaphor of his conversation with Secretary of Commerce Hoover, he wrote that Coolidge addressed the newspapermen as if he was president of a corporation. Desiring to be "a little malicious," which for Sullivan was not difficult, he amended his remarks and said Coolidge was like the chief clerk of a corporation.[33] The proceedings as he noticed them typically opened with the president sitting at his desk smiling and swinging his horn glasses until the crowd was in. He rose to face the reporters. The president referred to the little group as "the class," treating them as pupils. They could not quote him, and so invented "the White House spokesman," whom newspaper readers gradually recognized as Coolidge. In 1927 the president held what he described as an "executive session" of the conference and told the class to stop writing about the White House spokesman. He held them under classroom discipline. They had to submit questions in advance. If he did not like the questions, he forgot to answer them. One time he liked none of the questions: the class watched in dismay as each slip of paper, held in the presidential hand, fluttered down on his desk, after which he said without a smile, "I have no questions today." The class resorted to colored slips. It made no difference.[34]

A presidential activity that consumed far more time than the press conferences, requiring day after day rather than twice a week, was the writing of letters. To this task Coolidge again brought his prime administrative rule. Harding had dictated many letters, some quite long, but Coolidge hardly ever wrote one. He would sit at his desk, feet in a drawer, smoking a Havana (he kept the good gift cigars and gave White Owls to visitors) and annotating letters. These sentiments the presidential staff translated into suitable answers. Sometimes comments were brief, such as "yes" or "no." President John Grier Hibben of Princeton University wrote to invite the president to receive an honorary degree. At the top of the letter, in the unmistakable rounded hand and black ink, was a single word: "Sorry." The headmaster of Mercersburg Academy, W. M. Irvine, Ph.D., L.L.D., at whose institution the Coolidge sons were in attendance, began to write chatty letters, and the president wrote on one of them, "Always glad to hear from you. C." When Irvine died in 1928, Coolidge wrote on a letter from the Mercersburg alumni association, "yes prepare letter C."[35]

Much of the president's routine was ceremonial. At 12:30, six days a week, he shook hands with an average of four hundred tourists. Sometimes he spoke to them: "Mawnin." Former President Taft, watching at an evening reception, described all this as "pump-handle work," in which, he said, Coolidge showed neither grace nor enthusiasm.[36] But he did it because he was too wise a politician not to. If he was too busy to shake hands, he would have the door opened to the presidential office, and people could file by and catch a glimpse of their tax dollars at work.

Luncheons usually were reserved for important visitors and gave no opportunity for relaxation. After luncheon the president in good weather went out on the grounds and posed for photographs with groups; in bad weather he handled photographs in the public rooms.

The science of public relations was rising during the Coolidge era, with encouragement from bond sales during the recent war, and the president did what he could to advance himself within its measurements. In 1924 he allowed the Republican national committee to employ the self-styled "public relations counsel" Edward L. Bernays to humanize him. It is not certain what Bernays did, but the president began to manage extravagant things, such as a White House breakfast for a group of New York theatrical people, after which they adjourned to the garden where Al Jolson led the guests in a song—"Keep Coolidge!"—about voting for Coolidge.

> The race is now begun
> And Coolidge is the one,
> The one to fill the presidential chair.
> Without a lot of fuss
> He did a lot for us.
> So let's reciprocate and keep him there.
> (Refrain)
> Keep Coolidge! Keep Coolidge!...[37]

The guests and Mrs. Coolidge joined in the song. The humanizing must have worked, for Coolidge that year received a massive majority. After Bernays departed, the president continued to develop in this regard. During his western vacation in 1927, he not merely received a gift of a cowboy outfit from the Boy Scouts of South Dakota, bearing the initials C.A.L. down the leather sides, but he put it on—he wore it. Similarly a tribe gave him an Indian headdress and inducted him into their midst as Chief Leading Eagle. During the subsequent war dances the president sat in his allotted place watching the proceedings, wearing the headdress.

In conclusion it is of interest to remark—but no more so than of other aspects of Coolidge's personality or the extraordinary administrative abilities he showed in his high office—that the purpose of his life in politics was to serve the nation's, and before that his city's and state's, needs.[38] When he was governor of Massachusetts he related the point to Morrow, who had solicited his opinions about the theories of the Yale political economist William Graham Sumner. Morrow had sent him four volumes by Sumner. Whether Coolidge read them was questionable, although the governor told Morrow he read most of them. He said he regarded Sumner as on the whole sound. He took exception to the claim that human existence was on the basis of dollars and cents "as he puts it." Sumner contended that economic principles came first, thereafter democracy. He had little use, Coolidge wrote, for philosophy and religion. Then the telling comment: "He nowhere enunciates the principle of service."[39]

Service was the key to Coolidge's long public career. The purpose of his participation in government, from the first political move, which was to run for the Northampton city council in 1898, was that the citizen had an obligation to serve. The most important area of service was politics, which held society together. Coolidge did not believe, as did the Republican Roosevelt, that his task was housecleaning. It was not to sound alarm. His work in government was to follow the Constitution and the laws and carry out—to serve—the will of the people. It was a noble task, and by and large he accomplished it.

Five

THE UNITED STATES IN
WORLD AFFAIRS

1919–1945

JOHN A. Garraty: Professor Ferrell, how did World War I affect the average American's conception of the role that the United States should play in world affairs?

Robert H. Ferrell: I think it affected it adversely. Around the turn of the century and perhaps until 1914, there was a good deal of uncollected idealism in the United States, but unfortunately this idealism then came to nothing during World War I. People misconstrued the events of the war and the purposes of the European allies and rather quickly decided that the American war effort was not going to solve European problems. In fact, this idealism came to less than nothing because it turned into a dislike of Europe and anything that came from Europe.

One could almost argue that if the United States had not gotten into World War I it might have done some things more constructive for the peace of Europe. It might have involved itself with the political problems of Europe that were the essential problems, and perhaps helped to solve them. Instead, we produced a series of advices and programs that the Europeans didn't need, but sometimes took simply to please us.

J.A.G. I'm not sure I understand what you mean by European political problems.

R.H.F. Europe's problems were problems of power—of boundaries, of economic relations, of using force to preserve peace. Americans didn't want to touch these problems after 1918.

J.A.G. Was this attitude a product of the war itself, or of the controversy over the Versailles Treaty and American entry into the League of Nations?

R.H.F. Mainly of the war. The Versailles Treaty, its rejection by the Senate, the problems of President Wilson—these things have engaged historians, and of course they engaged the American people, but I think it was the experience of two million American troops in France, this mass tourism, if you will, that disillusioned the nation about Europe. It had never happened before—the generality of Americans going to Europe. Previously, only the Boston and New York upper crust traveled in Europe, and they saw a very special part of Europe. Suddenly, two million soldiers from all over the country, Captain Harry Truman of Missouri being one of them, saw another, and in a sense the worst, part of Europe. This was not a pleasant experience.

J.A.G. What role do you think Wilson's idealism played in this reaction? Did his setting of exalted goals for the United States that could not be achieved influence it?

R.H.F. It's rather easy to point out Wilson's mistakes now. I think historians have especially enjoyed doing so because Wilson was himself a historian. He pitched his rhetoric too high. But one could argue that, if it were possible to erase Wilson from the equation, it might not have made much difference.

J.A.G. You say that the experience of American soldiers in Europe made them anti-European?

R.H.F. This is evident in whatever correspondence of the 1920s one picks up. The generality of manuscript collections in the Library of Congress bear testimony to it. Dislike of Europe is a common theme in all of this material.

J.A.G. Do you mean letters written by men who had served in the army?

R.H.F. Yes. I could start with my own father, and move from there rather easily to statements by Harry Truman—the short section in his memoirs about life in his battery, for example.

J.A.G. How did this differ from the "traditional" suspicion of European standards of morals and society that one finds in American writings as far back as those of Thomas Jefferson?

R.H.F. That's a good question. Jefferson saw France in the 1780s, and he never forgot it; if before he wrote that cities were sores on the body politic, after that he was sure they were. But there was an exaggeration of American criticism in the 1920s, a perhaps deeper conviction and certainly a more widespread one.

J.A.G. Is the historian's strategy of dividing Americans into interventionists and isolationists useful for understanding American policy between the two world wars?

R.H.F. This strategy of putting people into either one category or the other has its advantages. We cannot know or describe everything and show all its complexities, so we have to shear off some of the truth, I suppose, as we try to describe the past. Yet having said that categories are useful, I think we must be especially careful of the word *interventionist.* There were no interventionists in the sense in which we use that word today. Most so-called interventionists in the 1920s merely wished to apply moral force to the problems of Europe. Some might have been willing to use real force in the Far East (provided it wasn't very much force). But in Europe no one was ready to use military power or even economic influence. A few kind expressions together with much free advice (we like to give advice to Europeans), this was how these interventionists hoped to solve the problems of Europe. They were not willing to get into the problems of the balance of power in Europe, which essentially was the problem of Germany. They liked to think that the Germans had turned over a new leaf when they set up the Weimar Republic; the very fact of establishing the republic seemed sufficient, and we thought we had done something at that point and really didn't need to do any more. And I don't think intervention ran beyond advice-giving after that.

J.A.G. Are you saying, in effect, that everyone in America was an isolationist?

R.H.F. It would be better to say that there was a spectrum of isolationism. At one end stood those who believed that the less one had to do with Europe the better; on the other, those willing to join the League of Nations and particularly to participate in its various humanitarian projects. The interventionists of the 1920s and 1930s might now properly be called isolationists.

J.A.G. I'm not sure I understand.

R.H.F. I think that most Americans were, by present-day standards, isolationists.

J.A.G. If everyone was by modern standards isolationist, how, then, can one distinguish between isolationists like Senators Hiram Johnson and William E. Borah, and "isolationists" like Secretary of State Charles Evans Hughes?

R.H.F. Borah is perhaps the most interesting and maybe even the most representative man of the period. He was essentially negative. He always had some great proposal that he was about to advance, but he never quite advanced it. Meanwhile he enjoyed himself taking apart the going notions of the moment. For example, he was in favor of a league but not that league; he was in favor of a world court, but not the court that was proposed by the League of Nations.

Secretary of State Charles Evans Hughes was, I think, mainly a legalist. He contributed little beyond advancing the disarmament conference of 1921–1922. One could argue that his secretaryship was not his most important public service.

J.A.G. Some Americans in the 1920s wanted the United States to join the League of Nations; others were opposed. Some favored joining the World Court; others were opposed. Were these divisions simply ad hoc reactions to particular situations? Was there no underlying difference of worldview? If not, how can the two positions be defined?

R.H.F. I suppose that, having quibbled over words, I would argue that it's not very helpful to try to create new words. We might just as well live with the words *isolationist* and *interventionist,* understanding that they had a meaning which is not our present-day meaning.

J.A.G. Was the League of Nations in your judgment a good idea? Was the world, and especially the United States, ready for international cooperation to the extent that the league called for?

R.H.F. I think that it's entirely possible that if we had joined the League of Nations the league might have been the worse for it. Let me explain.

J.A.G. I wish you would!

R.H.F. The basic problem of Europe after the war was Germany, and a basic tension existed between the French and the British with regard to Germany. The British, to reduce their position to a street phrase, argued that if one was nice to the Germans they would be nice to you. The French believed that the best way to handle the Germans was to put the lid on them and let them live with some of their problems. I think that if we had gotten into the league we would have sided with the British. This, then, would have given the Germans a latitude in European affairs that in fact they only obtained in the 1930s. I would contend, and perhaps this is an anti-German view, that the Germans were so embittered by their loss of World War I that the success of Hitler or someone similar to him was only a matter of time, and that in retrospect the best policy toward Germany was to contain Germany, forcefully if necessary. If the United States had joined the league we would have had a Hitler a decade sooner.

J.A.G. To what degree was American foreign policy between the two wars influenced by domestic political considerations?

R.H.F. I think that the politicians of the 1920s and 1930s, when they turned to questions of foreign policy, rather accurately reflected the feelings of the American people, except that, being uncertain about what woman's suffrage would mean, they gave a little bit more weight and credence to the opinions of such people as Carrie Chapman Catt and other women peace leaders than their real influence deserved. Apart from that exaggeration, I think that politics generally reflected, almost mirrorlike, the state of opinion in this country on foreign affairs. I see little evidence that politicians made points in foreign policy for partisan political purposes.

J.A.G. Did economic interests influence the shape of foreign policy?

R.H.F. The question of the influence of economics on politics has been much debated. The Great Depression focused the attention of Americans on economic problems as never before in their history, and it became popular to attribute economic purposes to all sorts of actions that may not have been economic in purpose at all. Misapplying the feelings of the 1930s to the mood of the 1920s inspired a number of historical interpretations about the concern of the government for economic interests in foreign policy. Some historians insisted that Herbert Hoover turned the department of commerce into a machine for soliciting business abroad. They pointed out that the first commercial attachés were appointed in this period, whereas earlier the support that the state department gave to foreign commerce had been desultory and almost completely unorganized. One can grant this and yet say that the political purposes of the government were not much expressed through economic pressures. I don't think that people do large things for economic reasons, although they often do small things that way. I certainly don't see our policy abroad as being shaped by economics. There was, for example, much talk in the 1920s about the economic aspects of our policy in Latin America, notably in Nicaragua. But the major American investments in Latin America were in Cuba and Mexico. Only a few million American dollars were invested in Nicaragua. The revolution of the later 1920s in Nicaragua, which admittedly involved several thousand marines, had almost nothing to do with economics. It resulted from the well-intentioned effort of Nicaraguans and of the United States to rid the government of the awful political alternation that had been tearing the country apart ever since the nineteenth century. I've seen some correspondence in state department files which indicates that the presidency of Nicaragua was sold for $30,000 in 1925–1926. In that sense it was an economic arrangement, but I don't think there was anything more to it.

J.A.G. Was the Washington disarmament conference in 1921 a diplomatic triumph for the United States?

R.H.F. The Washington conference, considering what it did for the navies of Britain, the United States, and Japan, was, I think, a considerable success. Not only did it establish a reasonable ratio for the navies of the three great naval powers, but it also coupled this with political arrangements in the Far East. It brought Japan to a kind of judgment after fifteen or twenty years, during which the Japanese had been able to operate rather freely in the Far East. The Japanese had moved against the Chinese in 1894, and against the Russians ten years later. They had taken the German colonies in China in 1914. It was impossible to stop this expansion, while the war was going on. That was the purpose of the Washington conference. It was a marvelous combination of bringing Japan to account and achieving some helpful limitation in the number of battleships and aircraft carriers. Of course, the arrangement collapsed in the 1930s, beginning with the London conference in 1930. But in the context of the problems of the 1920s I think it was quite a successful conference. (One could even argue that it was the only successful disarmament conference we've ever participated in.)

J.A.G. It has been said in criticism of the settlement that the naval ratio agreement misled the American people, that while it gave the United States a larger navy than Japan, the particular 5:3 ratio assured Japanese domination of the Western Pacific—that in effect we were surrendering the

Philippines to Japan any time the Japanese really wanted to take them. What is your opinion of this line of reasoning?

R.H.F. It's true that the Philippines were vulnerable, but not as a result of the Washington disarmament conference. They were vulnerable from the moment we took them in 1898. The files of the war department are full of references to the fact that the American position in the Philippines was indefensible. This was a well-known fact before World War I. The 5:3 ratio made no difference.

J.A.G. Professor Ferrell, you have written an important book on the Kellogg-Briand Pact of 1928. Will you explain why this toothless attempt to outlaw war seemed so important to many people at that time?

R.H.F. After the First World War the American people were tired of involvement in Europe. In writing about this period most historians use the word Harding supposedly invented, *normalcy.* I suppose it's as good as any. Using this word, one can say that Americans chose to enjoy life. After all, they had a higher standard of living than any people had ever had up to that time. Nonetheless, there was considerable feeling that somehow we had not done what we should. Many Americans thought that while the Europeans were fooling with the League of Nations and generally pursuing their own rivalries (which the United States should of course keep out of), their country had some responsibility, which it was not undertaking.

Much unformed peace sentiment in this country was attaching itself to what I would say in retrospect were foolish ideas, such as the World Court, and arbitration and conciliation treaties. This sentiment gathered in 1927–1928 to support the proposal, first made by Aristide Briand of France, and then shrewdly amended by the state department, which we call the Kellogg-Briand Pact.

Secretary of State Frank B. Kellogg, who started the whole thing as a maneuver against Briand, came to think that what he was doing was of very large importance. President Coolidge was always lukewarm to the proposal, but he probably felt that it wouldn't hurt anyone and that he could go back to his fishing in the Black Hills.

Kellogg had for a short time the support of the almost united peace sentiment of the United States: the educators, the preachers, the League of Nations people. But six months after ratification of the treaty came the stock-market crash, whereupon Americans turned to other, perhaps more important, thoughts. In one sense, however, it really was a great treaty for its time because it marked the first serious American effort, apart from the intervention in the World War to amend the policies and perhaps the future of Europe.

J.A.G. Why did Kellogg think the treaty so important?

R.H.F. Kellogg was a man whom many contemporaries made fun of. He had been defeated for reelection to the Senate in 1922 by a dentist named Hendrik Shipstead. It was said, perhaps correctly, that Coolidge had been nice to Kellogg, first sending him as American ambassador to England and then making him secretary of state, largely because Kellogg had been nice to Coolidge when Coolidge was only a vice president and when other senators weren't paying much attention to him. Kellogg did not have a college education. He did not understand the mysteries of the French language. When he saw the phrase "M. Briand," he didn't know that "M." stood for "Monsieur." He used to go to a hairdresser in Washington to get his hair curled, and he was very proud of one lock of hair, which showed prominently in all his photographs. I suppose he thought he was a great man.

But Kellogg was a man of many fine qualities. He was not merely a good lawyer; he had been president of the American Bar Association in 1912. In the Progressive era he had been the trustbuster. He had, after all, sued the Standard Oil Company, and he had won. He knew not merely the law but the workings of American politics. Coolidge appointed him, I think, because Kellogg's views were largely those of Coolidge.

Why, then, did he go for such a fatuous proposition as the Kellogg Pact? I think he did so because of his age—he was over seventy—and his desire for greatness, for the public approbation that, in fact, came to him, I think that's the answer, but I want to add hastily that in many ways he was a great man.

J.A.G. You said earlier that the idea of the United States participating in the World Court was "foolish." Why do you think so?

R.H.F. The World Court was largely an American proposition. It was the reigning idea of American international lawyers, and it was pushed by Elihu Root, who had a large part in its establishment when the protocol was drawn up in 1920. But it was not important for the peace of the world. It could not apply to the grand political problems of Europe, or even those of the Far East or Latin America. It could apply only to disputes over tiny islands or small minorities, or boundaries of a minor nature.

I would argue that it was not worth the intense concentration that the peace people gave to it, and that American lawyers gave to it, and even American politicians.

J.A.G. Do you mean that opposition to the court rose out of a mis-apprehension of its importance? That people were opposed to it because they thought it was more important than it in fact was?

R.H.F. Yes and no. The same misconception that focused attention on it produced the enormous concentration of nitpicking by critics. Actually, the Senate accepted the court with five conditions, which the other members refused to accept until Root went to Europe in 1929 and persuaded them to do so. Whereupon the Senate turned the protocol down. But with or without conditions, the court was never important. I understand that even today it has practically no business.

J.A.G. Would you discuss American policy toward Latin America between the wars? Was there any significant change in the policies pursued by the United States?

R.H.F. I think there was a break, but not until the 1930s. As soon as the World War broke out it was clear that whatever influence Germany or any other possible enemy nation might have in Latin America was going to be finished by the war. Thus imperialism was no longer necessary. But during the 1920s withdrawal was slow. A nation cannot easily pull out of a complex situation merely because involvement is no longer necessary.

Policy was no longer based on strategic considerations. In the best sense of American national ideals, efforts to be helpful, to move Latin American nations along what seemed the road to good international behavior, were attempted. And of course these nations, realizing that the old strategic purpose and its implied tool, military force, no longer existed, took advantage of the situation.

The policy of the country was benign and well-wishing, but it was impossible to pull the plug and walk out. In 1928 Hughes told the Latin Americans as much in a speech—which he, in retrospect, thought the greatest act of his career. During a conference at Havana, Hughes said that the United States would not stand by while Americans were, as he put it, "butchered in the jungle." His remark was almost the last defense of intervention, whether for the purpose of imperialism as "protective" imperialism, or simply for maintaining a sort of missionary policy in Latin

America. In December of 1928, President-elect Hoover toured Latin America and made all sorts of declarations of nonintervention. (In some of these speeches he used the phrase *good neighbor,* and later claimed that he was the inventor of the good neighbor policy rather than Franklin D. Roosevelt.) The government early understood how times had changed after 1917–1918, and wanted to pull out but couldn't do so easily.

J.A.G. The United States certainly has vital strategic interests in the Caribbean area, interests which have repeatedly appeared to be threatened, most recently in the Cuban missile crisis of 1962. Looking back at the whole period since the Spanish-American War, could an argument be made that we should have been more frankly imperialistic? Would the United States, and perhaps even the Caribbean nations, have been better off if, after 1898, we had taken the entire Caribbean area directly into our orbit?

R.H.F. One can make a very good argument in favor of that. It has sometimes been made in the case of Nicaragua, where the United States intervened just enough to maintain order. This intervention was somewhat analogous to British activities in Egypt, where the British worked through the Egyptian bureaucracy and all the institutions of the Turkish rule. In India, on the other hand, they made major changes and their impact was much more constructive. If we had taken over the government of Nicaragua, more constructive results might have occurred. And the same principle may be applied to Cuba, to the Dominican Republic, and, in view of the regime there now, to Haiti. This is partly retrospective. Probably I'm suggesting what at the time was an impossible policy. But perhaps we should have done it.

J.A.G. What is your opinion of the record in foreign relations of the post–World War presidents, Harding and Coolidge?

R.H.F. Harding's reputation is in the throes of reevaluation because of the discovery after many years of his papers, but when the reevaluation is completed we may not know a great deal more than what we do now. Harding was not greatly interested in foreign affairs. I don't think he had any feeling for Europe at all. He was basically a small-town Ohioan—a person who liked to talk, who enjoyed the hustings, who liked to get out and, as he put it, "bloviate." Foreign affairs were outside his understanding. It has been said that he was in safe hands because of his secretary of state, Hughes. His own lack of initiative in foreign affairs I think limited Hughes, who, being a man of conservative instincts, usually hesitated to move very far because he knew that he would have to take Harding with him. So Harding's impress on foreign affairs was virtually nil.[1]

Coolidge, however, deserves much more credit than historians have given him, in both domestic and foreign policy. He did not advance any large policies beyond supporting Kellogg in the Kellogg-Briand Pact. His one personal essay was the Geneva Naval Conference in 1927, which ran for a few weeks in the summer and turned to nothing, and in fact embittered Coolidge about Europeans.

But if Coolidge was not much more adventuresome than Harding, he did understand the problems of the day. I think Coolidge was an intelligent man and well versed in European problems. He was not much of a letter writer; therefore, it's difficult to find out what Coolidge thought about things. But there is one place where his opinions have been recorded— his press conferences. These were meetings with the Washington press corps, a group of no more than a dozen persons in those days. He referred to these reporters as "pupils," and he would lecture them as a teacher lectures to a class. Whatever he said was not quotable unless he gave express permission. Verbatim transcripts of the conferences show that Coolidge expressed his views on all sorts of subjects in great detail, presumably without notes. I find extraordinary his knowledge of domestic and foreign affairs, judging from these transcripts.

Coolidge also had a feeling for how far one could go in foreign affairs without raising domestic complications. He was a man of great good judgment. He has always been credited as being a funny man. He was witty, but I think the wit really showed the keenness of his intellect. He doled out his humor in a sort of Vermont way that always had a purpose, and it showed, I think, the acuteness of his mind. He realized that for Europe the later 1920s were a much better era than the early 1920s. It looked as though postwar European problems were on the way to solution. Germany was recovering and apparently peaceable. In Italy, Mussolini at that time did not seem the malign creature he later became—he appeared to be confining his attention to such things as clearing up the Roman streets and trying to solve the traffic problem. Coolidge, viewing Europe in this Indian summer of its life, felt that it wasn't necessary to be much concerned with the Continent.

He certainly had a wonderful sense of knowing when to do nothing, which is not a typical American attribute. He assumed that many problems would solve themselves without action. This was his attitude in domestic affairs and likewise in foreign affairs. Maybe he was right with regard to the Europe of his time. It was the Depression that turned everything askew, and this, of course, he did not anticipate. But then even John Maynard Keynes himself, the great economist of the 1930s, had no idea of the importance of the Depression until well into the 1930s.

J.A.G. The first occasion when the question of acting to stop the aggression that eventually led to World War II came up was the Manchurian incident of 1931. What did the United States government do at that time and why?

R.H.F. Many publicists at the time, and many historians later, called the actions of the United States in the Manchurian crisis a turning point— that's the phrase they liked—in the course of world affairs. The usual argument is that if the United States had faced up to the Japanese more quickly, with force or the threat of force rather than with words, the Second World War would not have occurred. The contention is that the failure to stop the Japanese was a great object lesson to Hitler, who came into power a year and a half later, and to Mussolini, already in power and becoming dangerous. Mussolini then tried his "experiment" in Ethiopia, which met with no large objection, and then Hitler, seeing Japan and Italy so successful in their aggression, proceeded to capitalize on the situation in 1938.

If this argument is correct, one can contend that the United States perhaps touched off a series of events that led to war in Europe in 1939 and eventually to Pearl Harbor. But I think this was not quite the case. Some people argued at the time that it was possible to divorce the problems of the Far East from those of Europe; many more contended that any unresisted aggression was likely to affect Europe. The usual way of describing the situation was to say that anyone who thought that you could isolate aggression was being unrealistic and even stupid. But I believe that the problems of Manchuria, which the Japanese, in their own way, were trying to solve in 1931–1933, were not much connected to the problems of Europe, and that if the United States had better understood Japanese and Chinese affairs at the time, and had sensed what the mood of both of those governments in the early 1930s was, it might have made an arrangement in Manchuria that would have been quite acceptable for the Far East and would have had no repercussions in Europe. The tendency to equate the Far East and its problems with the problems of Europe was in this instance unfortunate.

Next, let us talk about what the United States did. Our policy, as we can now see from the documents of the state department, the diary of Secretary of State Stimson, and other papers, is clear enough. It passed through stages. When the incident occurred, the reaction of the American government was extremely cautious. There was a feeling that we ought to find out what was actually going on, to give the Japanese a chance to save face—to control their troops, was the way Stimson put it—and to bring the situation under the control of the Tokyo government rather than that of the supposedly mad militarists in Manchuria. This point of view lasted for several weeks. The government then attempted a rather difficult diplomatic maneuver, sending Charles G. Dawes to Paris to push the League of Nations Council, to which of course the United States did not belong, into some sort of action. Dawes failed, at least partly because he offered no specific plan for action, and the league merely sent an investigating commission, which it eventually persuaded the Japanese to accept. The investigating commission contained an unofficial American member, Major General McCoy. The assumption was that the Japanese would not move any more troops into Manchuria while the commission was in the Far East.

This Lytton Commission was appointed in early December of 1931 and did not report until the following October. Meanwhile, with the consent—or at least the tacit support—of the government in Tokyo, Japanese troops in Manchuria continued to advance. This led the American government to adopt a new policy. On January 7, 1932, Secretary Stimson announced what became known as the Stimson Doctrine. The United States would not admit the legality of any situation de facto or any treaty or agreement set up in violation of existing treaties and affecting China.

No sooner had we announced this doctrine than the Japanese began to attack Shanghai. Our policy then moved into a fourth stage, signalized by the publication of the so-called Borah letter on February 24, 1932. This was a blunt restatement of the traditional American position toward the Far East, established in the Open Door notes at the turn of the century. There must be no violations of the "territorial integrity" of China.

Finally, there was a fifth American policy shift, an effort to get Japan "convicted" in the League of Nations, to prove to the world through the vote of the league that the Japanese had done something they shouldn't have done in Manchuria.

Stimson, being a lawyer, thought that this would have great effect upon the Japanese. Instead, it led only to a scene in the League of Nations. When the league made its judgment, the Japanese simply stood up and walked out. (The chief Japanese spokesman, Yosuke Matsuoka, said that as Christ had been crucified on the Cross, so was Japan being crucified by the League of Nations. When Matsuoka passed through the United States en route to Tokyo, he told a reporter that this was not quite the case. The nations of the world, he said, had taught Japan poker, in the course of which tuition they themselves had picked up most of the chips. But after they had gotten most of the chips they pronounced the game immoral and took up contract bridge.)

I think that our policy was for the time not a bad policy, but it was not effective. When one finds that having done several things yields no result, I suppose one always wishes that he hadn't done anything at all. It's clear now that nothing short of military force would have stopped the Japanese, and this was politically impossible in the United States in the midst of the Depression. It was almost impossible ten years later in 1941. After all, it took an outright attack upon American territory to bring the United States into the war.

This being the case, it was perhaps a mistake to have done anything, but as for the accusation that by allowing the Japanese to go ahead in Manchuria we insured the success of Hitler—that's merely foolish. Europe had its own problems, which were not related immediately or even very remotely to the problems of the Far East. Manchuria itself was a very special situation. It was possible for certain Japanese actions to take place in the Far East without having any effect upon Europe. One could even argue that a man like Hitler would have done what he did no matter what the world had done about Manchuria.

J.A.G. You said that it was politically impossible for the United States to use force in 1931–1932 against Japan. Public opinion in America would not have countenanced that. Did the political situation change in any way when superficially similar situations developed in Europe, beginning with the Ethiopian crisis?

R.H.F. In the Manchurian crisis, the government of the United States acted with almost no reliable information. In fact, the details of all of Japan's policy are just beginning to come out now, as Japanese scholars are working through the archives. We didn't know why the Japanese acted the way they did. But with regard to European affairs, of course the purposes of Hitler and Mussolini and the causes of their actions were fairly well known. Nevertheless, from the Ethiopian crisis through the Austrian and Czechoslovakian and Polish debacles, the Americans showed even less willingness to act, even in terms of giving advice, than they had displayed during the Manchurian affair.

I'm not altogether sure why this was so. Perhaps the intense popular fear and dislike of European politics were responsible, perhaps the feeling that events had already passed beyond any control of the United States. It may have been a comfortable belief that the British and French could take care of the Germans in event of war. But the fact is that, as European politics cascaded into war, the United States did almost nothing.

J.A.G. Wasn't the American neutrality legislation in effect a policy related to events in Europe?

R.H.F. I suppose so, in the sense that dislike of European politics was formalized in these neutrality pronouncements. To have a "policy" of neutrality, no matter what, is, in effect, to have no policy.

J.A.G. Are you saying that in the Manchurian situation, where our national interest was relatively uninvolved, we had a positive policy, but that in the European crises, where our interests were much greater, we had no policy?

R.H.F. Yes. That sounds like a paradox and perhaps it is, but of course it would have been safer to intervene in the Far East, since, after all, the situation didn't have the possibility of turning on us—we thought. There's a dictum attributed to Alfred Thayer Mahan that seems—whether Mahan actually said it or not—to characterize aptly our policy at the turn of the century. In Europe, abstention; in the Far East, cooperation (presumably with the British); in Latin America, dominance.

J.A.G. Did the European powers react more forcefully against the aggression of Italy and Germany, considering how much more directly they were threatened, than they had against Japan in Manchuria?

R.H.F. In considering the actions of the European powers, one comes back to the conflict between the British and the French over Germany.

In the 1920s, the French policy prevailed because the French were more active in the League of Nations, but in the 1930s, perhaps tired of trying to contain Germany, France surrendered leadership to Britain—at the wrong time, as we now see it. The differences between the French and the British enabled the Germans to operate very shrewdly. The willingness of the British to give in to Hitler's early importunities was particularly unfortunate. It is wrong to say that the United States started the chain of events that led to 1939 by its reaction to the Manchurian crisis; it is much more accurate to say that the British began it in 1935 by making a naval arrangement with the Germans in direct violation of the Treaty of Versailles. This apparently convinced Hitler that anything he did short of war itself was likely to get the consent of the British and thereby the reluctant consent of the French. It was a most unfortunate thing. If there was one single event in the 1930s that opened the floodgates to Nazism, as Churchill put it, it was the Anglo-German naval agreement of 1935.

J.A.G. What is your opinion of Herbert Hoover's performance in foreign policy?

R.H.F. Hoover, a distinctly different personality from his two predecessors, was equally interesting. He has done himself a disservice by publishing the three volumes of memoirs, which he wrote on odd occasions after he left the presidency. There is an inflexibility in the memoirs, a waspishness that could not possibly raise his historical reputation. But the Hoover of 1929–1933 was a man of large qualities, and the man best prepared for the presidency, one might argue, since John Quincy Adams.

J.A.G. And also equally as unsuccessful a president as Adams?

R.H.F. Equally unsuccessful, yes, and perhaps for the same reasons. Many comparisons can be made between Hoover and Adams. Hoover worked very hard. It was said that he worked about eighteen hours a day, and this is probably no exaggeration. He turned his attention to all sorts of details of the government. He was a very efficient person. He installed a telephone switchboard in the White House, and it was his custom to keep in close touch with the leading officers of the government. Any official could expect at almost any time of the working day to have the phone ring and hear the White House operator saying that the president was on the wire, whereupon President Hoover would come on with some comment or question. Of course, this often did more harm than good, because it brought Hoover into all sorts of situations he should not, I think, have entered.

This was probably Hoover's worst mistake as president: failure to delegate authority. (Coolidge, incidentally, was a master at delegating authority.) Hoover had to do things himself. His penchant for detail hurt his presidential performance greatly. Cordell Hull once said that Hoover was a person of great vision; "He could see a mare's nest farther than any other living politician." With all of his qualities of mind (he was a very intelligent man) and with all of his experience not merely in American domestic politics but also in foreign affairs, he failed as president. He couldn't deal with novelties when they suddenly came upon him. The Great Depression was of course his greatest failure, but he failed also in foreign relations because he lacked the appreciation of Europe that his wide travels might have been expected to give him. He had a profound dislike of foreigners, particularly Frenchmen, but also, I think, of Europeans generally. He referred to Frenchmen, incidentally, as "frogs," the World War I term. I think it was his experience with the financial problems of Belgian relief, and then at the peace conference, that led him to this position. His experience before the war abroad, I might add, was largely in Asia, not so much in Europe.

J.A.G. He was in Europe during most of the war, however.

R.H.F. Right, but he emerged from the peace conference feeling that the Europeans had tried to do us in. I think he believed firmly in that old cliché, "Americans always win wars and lose peace conferences."

At any rate, when Hoover turned to foreign affairs he didn't seem to have much imagination. He would "carry forward," as he liked to put it, the policies of his predecessors. He continued efforts toward disarmament; he continued especially the idea of naval conferences. Beyond this he did not go. He did allow himself to be talked into the moratorium on international debts, and when that became an item of possible political importance he rather carefully attached his name to it. Yet this Hoover moratorium was essentially a negative policy, a policy of dealing with problems that had appeared prior to his administration and that were not solved simply by delaying them.

J.A.G. Would you comment now on President Franklin D. Roosevelt's conduct of foreign relations?

R.H.F. Roosevelt was in office for a little more than three terms, and while it's usually not profitable to discuss a president's actions in the framework of his terms of office, it so happened that his first term coincided with the period of preparation in European aggression. From 1933 to 1937, while the politics of Europe were moving in ways that hardly inspired confidence, there was still some hope that the peace of 1919 might prevail. In that period Roosevelt did almost nothing in foreign affairs other than to set on foot officially a policy toward Latin America that had been well in force prior to his accession. Most historians pick that phrase *good neighbor* out of his inaugural address, but it was just a chance remark; the expression, as Arthur P. Whitaker has shown, was used as far back as the early nineteenth century. It was just a piece of guff of a sort often expressed about Latin America. He did not really have an active policy even toward Latin America. It was the passive policy of nonintervention that had become feasible after the World War. The first Roosevelt administration was not a time in which he made any sort of international reputation. If anything, his reputation went down after his action at the London Economic Conference in 1933, which was a completely irresponsible piece of diplomacy.

Beginning in 1937, Roosevelt took a stiff position toward Japan's resumption of the Far Eastern war. Later, at least verbally, he began to stand against Hitler when Hitler went first into Austria and then into Czechoslovakia and elsewhere. But, until the summer of 1940, his policy was not much more than verbal. Only with the destroyers-for-bases deal with Great Britain, which, while not of enormous aid to the Allies in itself, promised large assistance, did he begin to move seriously against Germany. It's possible, in fact, to argue that, until 1937, and perhaps even through 1939, Roosevelt's German policy was largely like that of Great Britain.

One can sense even before the election of 1940 that Roosevelt had decided that as president he simply had to move into the European arena. Then—and historians have long pointed this out—with the Lend-Lease Act in the spring of 1941, he came down unmistakably on the side of the democracies. This was a very large business, the Lend-Lease Act, clearly the most important act of foreign relations of his administration down to American entrance into the war. And he followed Lend-Lease with a policy that, although pursued surreptitiously, was almost equally important; the business of convoying ships to Great Britain.

That convoying is an interesting phase of Roosevelt's handling of foreign relations. It showed him, it seems to me, at his very worst as a president. As James MacGregor Burns has pointed out in his biography of Roosevelt,

The Lion and the Fox, when FDR was pursuing a great idea or a great purpose he was almost irresistible, a wonderfully attractive national leader. But when the going was difficult, he was tempted to move sideways and become, as Burns puts it, the fox rather than the lion. The convoy issue brought out his worst qualities. There is no question at all that Charles A. Beard was correct in calling his policy deliberately deceptive. In *President Roosevelt and the Coming of the War* Beard brought together the almost extraordinary assertions of Roosevelt in the summer and early fall of 1941 about convoying. Roosevelt decided he had to convoy Lend-Lease materials; otherwise, they would simply be sunk in the Atlantic by German submarines. But he didn't know how to get public support for convoying without lying about it. So he lied. He invented something he called a "patrol," which was, he told the American people, something quite different from convoying. He said that a convoy and a patrol were analogous to a horse and a cow; they were different animals, even if people wanted to think they were the same animal.

This particular example of press-conference pleasantry or joshing, at which he was a master, was a piece of misrepresentation, to put it mildly. He followed this up with a series of other deceptions, the most notable of which was his description of the attack by German submarines on the destroyer *Greer* in the early autumn of 1941. The *Greer* had been pursuing a submarine and broadcasting the submarine's position. It was only in desperation that the submarine launched a torpedo or two at the destroyer. Nonetheless, Roosevelt then went on the radio. In this broadcast, which it almost hurts to read, he said that the *Greer* was carrying the mail to Iceland. He added some more irrelevancies and misrepresentations and then announced that he'd given the navy orders to sink all German submarines on sight. It was, I think, the worst act of his twelve-odd years as president.

It may be that if Roosevelt had told the American people what he was doing they would not have supported him. But I like to think that, on a great issue such as convoying, they would have gone along had Roosevelt set all the facts before them.

J.A.G. Much criticism has been leveled by historians at the neutrality legislation of the 1930s. Can anything good be said about this legislation?

R.H.F. I suppose, in view of our experience in the First World War and all the criticism that was leveled at Wilson because of his decision to stand firm for the right of Americans to travel aboard belligerent vessels, the legislation of twenty years later made sense. It was better to define what the American choice, if there was one, on neutral rights should be.

I suppose the legislation did, as historians have said, apprise the European powers of just where we intended not to defend our rights. This is the result of any sort of definition. And one can argue that we did ourselves a disservice by being too plain.

But I suppose I'm hedging. Perhaps I should merely say that I don't know whether any good results flowed from the neutrality acts. There was an inevitability about this legislation. It has usually been ascribed to the investigation of the Nye Committee of 1934–1936 into the causes of the First World War. I think that even had Senator Nye not held those hearings, only part of which concerned the neutrality issue, some kind of definition was almost certain to come as soon as war threatened to erupt in Europe.

Some historians have argued that Wilson chose to defend the right of Americans to travel on belligerent vessels because he knew or sensed that this policy sooner or later would get the United States into conflict, which they presume he desired. I don't think that's true at all. Wilson took what to his generation seemed the commonsense view of the situation. He naturally interpreted the rights of Americans as broadly as he could, and in view of the fact that there had never before been a submarine issue, he did what one would have expected him to do.

J.A.G. If there was a certain inevitability about the neutrality legislation, and if Roosevelt, after 1939, was convinced that the national interest required active intervention in the war, doesn't that throw certain doubts on your estimate of the effectiveness of a more candid policy with regard to convoying? Wasn't the risk of candor enormous?

R.H.F. I'm not sure. It's true that Roosevelt desired to see the United States in the war and was, by any detached view of the situation, more certain to get his way by doing what he did.

J.A.G. In other words, then, given the strong public sentiment for neutrality, a disingenuous policy was almost necessary.

R.H.F. Perhaps.

J.A.G. Do you feel that the Nye investigation had a large effect on the man in the street's feeling about European entanglements, or did it simply reinforce attitudes that were already very strong?

R.H.F. I'm sure the Nye investigation reinforced attitudes that already were strong. The investigation actually didn't turn up as much sensational evidence about war profiteering and "merchants of death" as Nye claimed.

J.A.G. When Roosevelt began to change his mind about intervening in the war, what sort of people agreed with him?

R.H.F. It is difficult to generalize, but persons who had traveled in Europe and who followed European affairs closely were the ones who took alarm, and many—those who had not tended to hold to the old attitudes— favored intervention.

Consider, as an example of the isolationist type, Senator Borah. He was chairman of the Senate Foreign Relations Committee from 1924 to 1933 and the leading Republican spokesman on foreign affairs thereafter. He had never been outside the United States, not even to Canada. So his knowl- edge of European affairs firsthand was nil. But ignorance did not prevent him from holding forth on the national interests and values of all the nations of the world he'd never seen.

J.A.G. Did partisanship have much to do with public attitudes? Does the fact that Roosevelt was a Democrat explain why the Republican Party seemed to be more isolationist than the Democratic in the 1930s?

R.H.F. Some wits said that the Pacific was the Republican ocean and the Atlantic the Democratic one, that the Republicans had been in power when we took an interest in the Far East at the turn of the century and the Democrats when we went to war in Europe in 1917. I suppose the person- ality of Roosevelt, dominating the Democratic Party, drove most of the isolationists out of that party, or at least put them off in a corner. And I suppose the need to oppose Roosevelt drove some Republican rhetoricians to statements that, when the chips were down, they were not prepared to back up. (During the election campaign of 1940, Wendell Willkie made a statement almost akin to Roosevelt's famous statement about not sending "our boys" into a "foreign" war. When he was asked about it later, he said it was simply a piece of campaign rhetoric, and dismissed it.) There were, though, many diehard isolationists, such as former President Hoover, in the Republican Party of 1940.

J.A.G. In what ways were the pressures that drew the United States into World War II different from those that led to American entry into the First World War?

R.H.F. I think that historians now generally agree that it was Wilson's defense of neutral rights that led us into the first war. In the Second World War, American entrance resulted, I think beyond question, from the hard line that the administration and the American people took toward the Japanese. The administration was not willing to allow Japan to expand in China, and the public backed it up. On November 26, 1941, the very day on which the Japanese attack fleet sailed for Pearl Harbor, Secretary of State Hull sent a note to the Japanese that virtually asked them to get out of China entirely, an impossibility considering their involvement there, which went back to 1894. This policy brought the Japanese to the decision to attack Pearl Harbor.

Of course, Roosevelt's measures in support of the French and British had won a good deal of popular approval; if there was not a complete support for his policy toward Europe, there was at least no chance of our supporting Hitler. Once the war with Japan began, it was a foregone conclusion that we would fight against Hitler too, and he settled the question by declaring war on us.

J.A.G. If Japan had not attacked Pearl Harbor, is it possible that we would never have entered the war in Europe?

R.H.F. I think it's entirely possible that we would not have gotten into the war until perhaps 1943, and perhaps we might have stayed out altogether. It's an interesting question, because had we not been dragged in by the debacle of Pearl Harbor, all of 1942 would have gone by without the sort of mobilization we needed to exert our strength in Europe, and if we had entered in 1943 we would not have had any effective forces available until 1945. By that time, the Russians probably would have rolled back the Germans—perhaps somewhat slower than in fact they did, but, nonetheless, they would have kept their juggernaut going, and they would have gone all the way to Gibraltar and taken over all of Europe, and presumably the British Isles with it. We would have been mobilized by that time, but it would have been too late to save Europe.

J.A.G. In other words, in your estimation the Germans would have lost whether we went into the war or not?

R.H.F. I think they could not have won against the Russians in view of what we know did happen. After all, up until 1944 and the invasion of France, the great bulk of the fighting was between the Russians and the

Germans, and by that time the Russians clearly were rolling the Germans back. The Germans just didn't have the population to stand against the Russians.

J.A.G. The question of Pearl Harbor is, of course, very controversial. Did Roosevelt want the Japanese to attack some American interest directly so that the question of getting into the war would solve itself?

R.H.F. Charles C. Tansill, who was a writer of quality on nineteenth-century American foreign policy, wrote a book, *Back Door to War*, which had as its theme the notion that Roosevelt, unable to open the front door to war, then tried with the back door. He took on the Japanese, who were not as clever as the Germans, and he maneuvered them into starting a war with the United States.

This is an ingenious but unbelievable thesis. For example, the cost of this "maneuvering" was the Pacific fleet. Roosevelt's great interest in and love of the navy, demonstrated by the many naval mementos at the Roosevelt Library in Hyde Park, suggests that he would have been the last person to sacrifice the navy even for a supposedly great end. Furthermore, any kind of a plot would have involved many persons, and someone would surely have let something out of the bag. I might add that those who accept the "back door" theory have never been able to find any concrete documentary evidence. All they have is circumstantial evidence, which in itself is quite interesting.

J.A.G. Well, of course there is a difference between saying that Roosevelt wanted Pearl Harbor attacked and saying that he wanted to create a situation where Japan would attack somewhere so that the United States could enter the war.

R.H.F. If you put the case that way, I think it's quite true that Roosevelt was ready for an attack by the Japanese somewhere. The first place he thought that they might attack was Malaya; the second place, Thailand; the third place, the Dutch East Indies; the fourth place, the Philippines; and the fifth—Pearl Harbor. The situation was like that of President Polk in the Mexican War. Polk was glad the Mexicans attacked because he wanted war. I think Roosevelt by December 1941 was convinced that the Japanese had to be put down—that it was impossible to try to prop the British up in Europe while the British empire was disintegrating in the Far East. Secretary Hull's note of November 26 to the Japanese was itself an apt expression of Roosevelt's feeling: Japan had just gone too far. The administration was ready for a Japanese war, and perhaps even invited one.

J.A.G. I still think that you're skirting around Tansill's argument. The American people were reluctant to get into a fighting war. If the Japanese had attacked Malaya or Thailand as you indicate Roosevelt expected, would it not still have been extremely difficult to get Congress to declare war? Whereas an attack on American territory would, as it did, solve Roosevelt's "problem."

R.H.F. The fact that they chose Pearl Harbor was not the first nor was it to be the last Japanese stupidity. They did it in a fit of logic. They figured that the Pearl Harbor fleet represented the largest and most dangerous force in the Far East that was hostile to them. They felt it had to be eliminated. It was a marvelous piece of logic, but it was very bad politics, because, as you say, even had there been an attack on the Philippines, Roosevelt would have had a devil of a time persuading Congress to declare war. I think that by late 1941 Roosevelt was willing to go to the Congress and ask for war, even if it did not involve American territory. But the fact is that the Japanese, with extraordinary foolishness, bailed him out by attacking Pear Harbor.

J.A.G. Can responsibility for the defeat at Pearl Harbor be laid on the shoulders of anyone "higher up" than the commanders on the scene, Admiral Husband E. Kimmel and General Walter C. Short?

R.H.F. Some years ago I wrote an article appraising the literature of Pearl Harbor, in which I defended Admiral Kimmel, who was still living. I sent a copy of the article to Kimmel, and the old man wrote back a rather primitively typed and spelled letter, in which he reiterated his feeling that the blame for the destruction of the fleet rested, as he put it, in Washington. He believed this, so far as I know, down until the time of his death. His book, *Admiral Kimmel's Story,* did not receive good reviews, but what is important is that he pointed out, cleverly—and, I believe, truthfully—that Pearl Harbor was indefensible in 1941; that his predecessor, Admiral James O. Richardson, had told Roosevelt this; and that Roosevelt had fired Richardson as a result. Kimmel was doing his best to make the place defensible, but almost no American position in the Pacific was defensible in December 1941. It was Kimmel's bad fortune that the Japanese chose Pearl Harbor.

General Douglas MacArthur in Manila was much more culpable than the commanders in Pearl Harbor because MacArthur had several hours of warning and, despite this warning, lost his touted B-17 bombers, which were sitting on the ground. MacArthur, in a rather undignified manner, passed the blame to subordinates, and the question of responsibility was fudged, but it was not fudged at Pearl Harbor. Kimmel and Short were virtually forced into retirement. It was a disgraceful episode, and General George C. Marshall later admitted manfully that he bore some of the responsibility for what had happened. Roosevelt never did admit to any responsibility. I feel very sorry for Kimmel. I think the responsibility ran all up and down the chain of command, and it probably reached well beyond that, into Congress, and probably to the American people.

J.A.G. Do you have any thoughts about the breaking of the Japanese code and the extraction of information about the Japanese plans for Pearl Harbor?

R.H.F. Failure to use this intelligence at the time of Pearl Harbor was one of the great intelligence failures of the United States. The direct result was the creation of the Central Intelligence Agency six years later. After we got into the war, the army and navy repaired that mistake by winning at Midway an intelligence victory by using the code. The military later shot down Admiral Isoroku Yamamoto through this same code. Indeed, we read Japanese messages down until the end of the war. But on the initial occasion when the code should have been used, we failed miserably.

J.A.G. How is Roosevelt's place in history affected by his performance as a diplomat during the war? For example, he is said to have had a penchant for personal diplomacy. Would you comment on his relationships with the great foreign leaders with whom he dealt, Churchill and Stalin?

R.H.F. Roosevelt's relations with these two men, Churchill and Stalin, were complex. When he first met Stalin at Tehran, he simply tried to impress his personality upon Stalin. The American war effort had not produced much of consequence in Europe as yet. There being no large, current issues between the two countries, it was a fairly successful meeting.

But at Yalta, when things got more concrete, the president found that he could not get altogether what he wanted from Stalin. He had to give on some things, and it doesn't seem that the good personal relations established at Tehran produced anything of moment. It would be difficult to show that Stalin gave in to the American president just because of any personal aura that Roosevelt created at either of these meetings.

His relations with Churchill, while still not yet entirely clear, were fascinating. Someone should write a book entitled *Roosevelt and Churchill*.[2] Their relations were, despite superficial cordiality, in the main uneasy. Churchill was too great a man, too properly calculating of the interests of Great Britain, to allow personal feelings to obtrude when he dealt with Roosevelt. He had to put up with a great deal from Mr. Roosevelt. Roosevelt liked to twit him about India and about the British empire, and he liked to give him advice on all kinds of subjects on which Churchill was in fact much more experienced. Churchill was himself an advice giver of some note, and when he had to take advice from Roosevelt, it must have been one of the most difficult experiences of his career. But advice he did take, and he seems to have been very careful not to say anything personal about Roosevelt. This was one of the great marks of Churchill's quality as a statesman.

As the war progressed, and as the American contribution became larger and larger, Roosevelt liked to put himself in the position of mediating between the British and the Russians. This Churchill detested, as well he might have. But he didn't say anything, in order to preserve the friendship, which of course was the right thing to do.

J.A.G. Do you think that Roosevelt was too reliant on personal relationships?

R.H.F. I suppose so. The differences between the Americans and the Russians were potentially so large that no amount of personal glossing could have covered them. Roosevelt might have had more success had he allowed some of these problems to come up more quickly and then dealt with them. He followed a policy in itself quite supportable, that larger diplomatic questions ought to be postponed until the end of the war. Victory was the important thing. But it might have been better to have allowed some of those disagreements to emerge in 1943–1944. Whether we could have then used our army in 1944 to counter some of the Russian demands, I'm not so certain, but at least the disagreements would have been out in the open. Then, perhaps, the postwar disillusion would have been less intense.

J.A.G. What were Roosevelt's hopes or intentions for a settlement after the war?

R.H.F. Roosevelt did not have a philosophical mind. He liked to deal with concrete problems. He felt that the problems of peace were essentially postwar. He felt also that the American troops would be withdrawn from Europe and probably that we could not do much about postwar Europe.

J.A.G. Was American foreign policy from 1919 to 1945 realistic or idealistic, in the sense that these terms have been used by historians such as Robert Osgood and George Kennan?

R.H.F. Ever since George F. Kennan published his remarkable book *American Diplomacy* in 1951, students have been talking about realism and idealism, and splitting these philosophical hairs. Robert E. Osgood, in a less known but equally important book, *Ideals and Self-Interest in America's Foreign Relations* (1953), has made the same point about idealism and realism. But I think both of these works obscure the realities of foreign policy. All life is a combination of ideals and interests. To paraphrase Jefferson—we are all realists, we are all idealists. One simply cannot separate these things.

If one looks at the history of American policy in the twentieth century, it is possible to argue that there has on occasion been more ideal than interest in foreign policy, that only since World War II has American policy displayed a reasonable combination of ideals and interests, a bringing together of power and diplomacy. It is foolish to ask: "Are we realists or idealists?" Where I disagree with both Kennan and Osgood is that I think we have to be both, whereas they think we should be, as they put it, realists. If one deals with the American public, one has to talk in ideals. There have to be doctrines. Except for John Kennedy, every president since Roosevelt has had a doctrine—the Truman Doctrine, the Eisenhower Doctrine.

J.A.G. What is your view of the so-called revisionist school of diplomatic historians?

R.H.F. One of my revered teachers, Harry R. Rudin, said years ago—and it's a point I like to remember—that we are all, as historians, revisionists, that we have to separate what happened from what people thought happened, and that the thought often gets quite remote from the actuality. The revisionists of the historiography of the First World War performed a useful task when they pointed out that what the nations said in 1914 and before was not always what they were doing. The publication of the documents in the 1920s, first by the Germans and then by the other leading powers, gave historians a field day, and they rewrote the history of the First World War. Their history was not always completely, shall we say, realistic, but it certainly showed aspects that contemporaries never even imagined had existed. But the fact that revisionists proved useful in regard to the First World War was picked up by a group with different purposes with regard to the Second World War. These people were in essence Roosevelt haters, determined to show that Roosevelt not merely moved the country toward socialism but also took it into an unnecessary war. These revisionists have merely obscured the historical record.

J.A.G. What is your opinion of the "new left" interpretation of the diplomatic history of this period?

R.H.F. The new left writers, most of them comparatively young men, are also revisionists, and in the sense that all history is revision I think we need these new interpretations or investigations. Insofar as the new left writers have looked at foreign policy, they have read the present, especially the problem of Vietnam, into the past. They are concerned mainly with the mistakes of American policy. They believe that the prime mistake was getting out of tune with the Russians in 1945–1946. Gar Alperovitz, for example, in his book *Atomic Diplomacy,* argues that the Americans dropped the two atomic bombs on the Japanese not to destroy two supposedly military targets and hasten the end of the war in the Far East, but to overawe the Russians and gain leverage in the postwar era.

Alperovitz makes a good case. He writes well. He moves easily in his discussion from point to point. But when he leaves the evidence and presents his conclusion, one discovers that the evidence has not quite proved his point, which is actually unprovable, at least from the research materials currently available.

But I would like to make a general point about the new left history as it applies to twentieth-century subjects. There has been a great proliferation of historical materials available for research. There has been an enormous keeping of records. We have so many documents that it is impossible to read them all. The young historian just coming out of graduate school, terribly anxious for a book, or at least an article, wanting something that will advance his fortune in the profession—a profession that is bouncing in terms of income and possibilities for promotion—the young historian, having been told by his graduate teachers that he must have an idea or thesis, and having learned also that it is possible to plunge into the morass of research materials and come out with something resembling support of almost any thesis, can put together a rather convincing, or at least plausible, argument that may not have much relation to history as it happened. I won't say that one can prove anything by documents. But most of the documentary sources are opinions. If one takes the opinions on the side he wishes to support, he can put together an argument.

I think that the new left, worried about America's moral stature and distrusting the present government, has produced literature based largely on this type of use of source material.

J.A.G. That raises a very interesting question. Even if we accept what you say about the motivation of the new left historians, how can the historian of modern foreign relations deal with the unreadably large body of conflicting evidence? What can the honest historian do if he cannot truly master the sources and yet still wishes to be objective?

R.H.F. It's absolutely true that the historian cannot read all the sources. I've had the experience of sitting down with great masses of state department files and trying to sort out what seems to be repetitive or trivial from the materials that seem to be the heart of controversy. I don't have any solid advice in this regard. There isn't much that one can say, other than to ask the historian always to be willing to change his mind, to try to use common sense toward the material. One must always ask himself how close he is getting to the truth, and whether he has seen what appears to be the most important information. I think the new left has instead tried to score points, set up their objectives.

Woodrow Wilson.

President Woodrow Wilson delivers his inaugural address, March 5, 1917.

The inauguration of Warren G. Harding, March 4, 1921.

Harding and "the little fellow," as he described Vice President Calvin
Coolidge.

The president's office in the West Wing, as Coolidge knew it. A disastrous fire on Christmas Eve 1929 burned almost everything or led to its ruin with water from the fire hoses. The result was the Oval Office.

President Hoover looks away, on inaugural day, as his successor looks ahead.

The chairman of the Democratic convention in Chicago, Senator Samuel D. Jackson of Indiana, July 21, 1944, holds up the hand of the party's nominee for vice president in the November election.

Former president Truman addressing a group of high school students at the Truman Library in Independence, listening to a question.

$\mathscr{Six}$

HARRY S. TRUMAN

*A Chance President in
the New World of Superpowers*

I f D U R I N G his third term President Franklin D. Roosevelt ever thought that the junior senator from Missouri, Harry S. Truman, would be his successor in the White House, FDR would have put the thought out of his mind. Truman would have done the same—until, that is, he received the vice presidential nomination at the Democratic national convention in Chicago in 1944. Truman was sixty years old in May of that year and as late as July 19 could not be sure that the lightning would strike.

Over the next years, with Truman serving nearly two full terms in the White House and asked to resolve the most baffling problems not merely in domestic but especially in foreign policy, the thirty-third president did well. It is indeed possible to contend not only that the former Missouri senator was perhaps number eight in the pantheon of the presidency, but also that he may even deserve, as the years pass and judgments sharpen, to be counted as the nation's second best president, behind only Lincoln.[1] The latter saved the Union, preserving it for survival into the present twenty-first century. Truman's principal task, which he managed with occasional errors but for the most part with aplomb, was of nearly equal importance: he turned the foreign policy of the country from isolation and occasional intervention in the affairs of Europe to a necessary participation

117

in world affairs. In this respect, one should add, he may not have possessed the remarkable wisdom and clear understanding of the need for national unity that President Washington had, the intellectual acuity of Jefferson, the almost overwhelming sense of national purpose that Jackson brought to the White House, the moral certainty of Wilson, or the grand-seignorial ability to preside over the Great Depression and a great war as Franklin Roosevelt did. He was capable of forays into hotheaded intemperance. With advancing years he was beginning to lose his "bounce," his quick ability to react. He did not always know that lack of formal education beyond the Independence High School class of 1901 had ill equipped him for some of the requirements of representing the whole nation. He did not sense that he put too much trust in subordinates and that some of them could deceive him. But he had an acute feeling for the need to pursue greatness, not for himself but for the whole country. When people asked if he considered himself a great president, he would say that he never considered himself that way but that he had a great time trying to be great. With his assemblage of qualities, he by and large rose to the challenges of his time. By defining foreign policy for the next half century and more, he made himself—not in a personal way but for what he managed to do for the country—a great president.

1

The nomination of Truman for vice president in 1944 was the most extraordinary political arrangement of the twentieth century. Its details were not well known and have remained so through the years. It was an underhanded, furtive business, not a great credit to the management of American politics as a whole, although the result was good, and perhaps what turns out all right is all right.[2]

The foundational problem was that President Roosevelt was coming apart physically due to cardiovascular disease. When the resident cardiologist at Bethesda Naval Hospital, Lieutenant Commander Howard G. Bruenn, first saw the president on March 28, 1944, he discovered that Roosevelt's condition was, as he related many years later, "God-awful." He knew it the minute he and his assistants lifted the president up on the table and Roosevelt was short of breath.

In subsequent weeks and months the blood pressure readings told the essential story. Bruenn placed a few readings in an article he published in 1970, and others are in the Roosevelt papers at Hyde Park. In 1941 the president's systolic pressure had been 170, the diastolic 110. Throughout 1944–1945 readings rose and fell but without exception were dangerously high and on occasion shockingly so. In November 1944, after the election, Roosevelt went to Warm Springs, Georgia, and went in the pool and thoroughly enjoyed himself. After he came out, Bruenn took his pressure, and to his horror the systolic was 260. It was the last time the president went in the pool. When he died on April 12, 1945, his systolic was 300.

It was an impossible condition. In a time before blood pressure pills, there was nothing for a physician to do except prescribe rest, which was difficult for the president of the United States. Bruenn resorted to digitalis, which was a palliative; it made the patient's heart work better, but there was nothing that could be done about its basic weakness, which Bruenn in his initial examination described as heart failure.

The Bethesda cardiologist became in effect Roosevelt's personal physician for the last year or so of the president's life. Vice Admiral Ross T. McIntire, the navy's surgeon general, had been FDR's personal physician since 1933 and had been misdiagnosing him, believing that he suffered from a nasal drip and from a hacking cough—bronchitis, he defined it—and that was true enough but only the beginning of the symptoms. Bruenn was a heart specialist; he had been at Columbia Presbyterian before the war and after the war went back to New York City and developed a large Park Avenue practice. McIntire was a graduate of a predecessor of the University of Oregon Medical School before World War I and for years had been a navy administrator.

The leaders of the Democratic Party did not know anything about Dr. Bruenn's diagnosis but knew from Roosevelt's appearance that he was in trouble. He was losing weight. At the Tehran Conference in November–December 1943 he suffered gastric pains that probably were a gallbladder attack. There were two more such episodes when he went to Bernard Baruch's estate in South Carolina in April–May 1944 to enjoy what became four weeks away from Washington. Actually the weight loss was a good thing. Bruenn had put him on a diet because his weight was 180 pounds; all of it was in his shoulders and stomach, his hips and legs having atrophied because of the infantile paralysis he contracted in 1921. As for the gastric upsets, the doctor put him on a bland diet, and they disappeared. The signs therefore were unrelated to the basic cardiovascular problem. But they alerted the party leaders, who from their own diagnoses (there was talk of cancer) drew the conclusion that the president was a very ill man.

The party's leaders decided that something had to be done: the need was to arrange a successor. Here arose a difficulty with the current vice president, Henry A. Wallace. The leaders did not like Wallace, who had run only once for office, in 1940—for vice president. Furthermore, he was a liberal, and they hardly knew what the word meant; they would not have called themselves conservatives, but they did not like liberals. In addition, Wallace did not have any kind of support in the South. How could the party run such a man as the vice president without losing votes? Moreover, and this was their principal objection, they did not want him in the presidency when Roosevelt died.

One should add that it was impossible to tell the president that he should choose a successor. In the way of cardiovascular patients, Roosevelt tired easily but felt fine; he was not at all aware of how ill he was. He was in full possession of the power of the presidency, and any hint that the leaders were looking to his succession could have banished them into outer political darkness. It was not possible to talk with him on this subject.

The result was a veritable conspiracy to get Wallace out of the vice presidency. It was led by the treasurer and secretary of the party, an oil man from California, Edwin W. Pauley, who one day while in the president's outer office in the West Wing "had a huddle with Pa," the president's appointments secretary, Major General Edwin M. (Pa) Watson. The two decided they would bring into the Oval Office those individuals who were likely to become delegates to the national convention, and these people (whom they made certain were anti-Wallace) would tell the president how poor a candidate the vice president would be.

Pauley and Watson brought into their group the postmaster general, Frank C. Walker, a quiet, inconspicuous man, one of the original Roosevelt supporters in New York City in 1932.[3] They brought in George E. Allen, who took over Pauley's office as party secretary, with Pauley retaining the treasurer's office; Allen was an amusing fellow who later published a book entitled *Presidents Who Have Known Me*. In addition, the Pauley group included Robert E. Hannegan, chairman of the national committee, who had grown up in St. Louis and in 1940 provided eight "delivery wards" for Truman in the very tight senatorial primary when Truman was fighting for his political life against Governor Lloyd C. Stark; Hannegan produced eight thousand machine votes in an election when Truman's plurality in the state was less than eight thousand.[4] Another confederate in the anti-Wallace group was the boss of the Bronx, Edward J. Flynn.

The purpose of the conspiracy was to convince Roosevelt that Wallace would hurt the ticket and even bring defeat against the Republican Party's very able standard-bearer, Governor Thomas E. Dewey of New York. Gradually the group persuaded the president that Wallace had to go. A sign appeared in May 1944, when the vice president asked to undertake a mission—he enjoyed going abroad, representing the president—to Russia. Roosevelt instead proposed that he visit China, via Outer Mongolia, and on his return pass through Siberia. After Wallace left the Oval Office it was almost apparent that the president was delighted to get his vice president out of the country during the crucial weeks before the Chicago convention. One had to suspect that the president, who enjoyed quips, probably told visitors, "I sent Henry to Siberia."

About this time, with Wallace on the trip to East Asia but hoping against hope for renomination, another contestant for the vice presidency (read: presidency) appeared, and this was the president's "assistant president," as FDR described him, James F. Byrnes, who was a former congressman and senator from South Carolina and in 1941–1942 served as associate justice of the Supreme Court. Ambitious, bright, but carrying the political burden of his state (that is, having to support over the years his state's and section's racial views), he would not have been able to achieve national office unless sponsored, and the vice presidency hence attracted him. He bore another political burden, which was that he once had been a Catholic but had given up Catholicism upon marriage, going over to his wife's Episcopalianism. Again, this burden would be no problem if he was sponsored for national office.

But Roosevelt noticed Byrnes's ambition and began to play with him, in a series of subtle ways, willing to use him momentarily as an alternative to Wallace—but how far he would have gone with Byrnes at Chicago was at the time and remains a mystery.

Such was the situation when the president asked the leaders to assemble in the White House for dinner on the evening of July 11, a Tuesday, eight days before the opening of the convention. The dinner was to be followed by discussion and presumably a choice of the vice presidential candidate, although, to be sure, the president and the leaders would go through the charade of not desiring to dictate to the convention and leaving the delegates to choose the ticket.

The meeting gave the appearance of a decision. Before dinner the president mixed the martinis, and Pauley in his later description of what happened remarked that the leaders—Pauley, Walker, Allen, Hannegan, Flynn, Mayor Edward J. Kelly of Chicago—all complimented him on their excellence. Roosevelt liked to be complimented on anything he did. After dinner the group assembled in the blue oval room next to the president's bedroom and quickly eliminated not merely Wallace but also Byrnes, and the choice began to point to Truman. The president summed up the sentiments of the meeting by turning to Hannegan and saying, "Bob, I think you and everyone else want Truman." Memories differed, but everyone present agreed he said something of the sort.

The president, as was his wont whenever there was bad news, asked his assistants to deliver it, and so he parceled out two principal tasks, with Hannegan to see Wallace the next day, and Walker to see Byrnes. On Wednesday morning the two bad-news deliverers performed their tasks. The recipients then took positions that were marvelous in the sense of how they had prepared themselves for what they may have anticipated. Wallace and Byrnes said, in effect, that they could not believe the messengers were delegated by the president and that FDR must deliver the news himself. They knew that Roosevelt would never deliver such news. Having learned that he did not want them, they defied him. Both knew the nomination meant the presidency.

In the business of keeping the president off balance, Wallace, who had returned from East Asia on Monday morning, July 10, spent a great deal of time with him, attempting to pin him down about the vice presidential nomination. The vice president saw the president the very afternoon of his return and lunched with him the next day and also on Thursday.

Byrnes also pressed the president unmercifully. On Thursday morning, before Wallace's lunch, he spent an hour in the Oval Office arguing his availability, opposing Wallace. Byrnes's close friend, Leo T. Crowley, who was head of the Foreign Economic Administration, undertook to represent the South Carolinian and was in and out of the Oval Office. Early

Friday morning Byrnes carefully called Truman, who was in Independence, and just getting his automobile out of the barn in back of his house, preparing to drive to Chicago. Byrnes asked the senator to nominate him at the convention. There had been talk that Truman might receive the nomination, although he was saying that he was not a candidate, and in this way Byrnes put him on the spot and, it appeared, eliminated him. Afterward Byrnes lunched with Hannegan and Walker, and when the postmaster general repeated his remarks of the previous Wednesday and Hannegan backed him up, Byrnes said he did not believe them and that he would call the president, who by that time was in Hyde Park. Roosevelt had taken the train to Hyde Park the night before and was leaving Friday evening for the West Coast, whence he would take ship for Hawaii to converse with his Pacific commanders concerning the war's strategy. Byrnes got through to the president just as Roosevelt was getting up, having rested. He asked him if it was true that Truman was in, Byrnes out. The president's answer, a remarkable half-truth, maybe a full-blown lie, was, "I did not say that I preferred anybody or that anybody would cost me votes; but they all agreed that Truman would cost fewer votes than anybody. . . . This was the agreement they reached and I had nothing to do with it. I was asking questions. I did not express myself." He said that of all the people mentioned for vice president, he, Byrnes, was his closest friend.

Over the following weekend, Friday, July 14, through the following Monday, July 17, horrendous confusion ensued in Chicago as Hannegan met the president's train in the rail yards on Saturday, July 15, and learned that Byrnes was acceptable. Byrnes himself entrained for Chicago. Gradually a condition that the president placed on Byrnes's candidacy when talking with Hannegan—"Clear it with Sidney" (the vice president of the Congress of Industrial Organizations and head of the CIO's political action committee, Sidney Hillman)—made his nomination impossible. Whether Roosevelt, who had seen Hillman the preceding Thursday, instructed the labor leader to say no to Byrnes is impossible to know, but it does look that way.

Byrnes was turned down on Monday, July 17, after Hannegan and Mayor Kelly arranged for signs reading "Roosevelt and Byrnes" and after the sign painters talked to reporters. Byrnes, pushing hard, had asked the president of the CIO, Philip Murray, for support, and Murray said he was for Wallace but would not oppose Byrnes. Murray seems then to have

talked with Hillman, who refused to support Byrnes, describing him as
antilabor, this because Byrnes in 1943 in his role as assistant president
had issued a "hold the line" order against raising hourly wages, at that time
set by government regulation. Moreover, when Ed Flynn that afternoon
arrived from New York and learned that Byrnes was the momentary choice
for vice president, he refused to believe it. The confusion forced the leaders
to call Roosevelt, then on his train proceeding toward San Diego. The leaders asked him who he wanted. The president, one suspects, was waiting for
the question. Speaking to Walker, he said, "Frank, go all out for Truman."

David McCullough has written that Flynn, who raised the fuss against
Byrnes among the leaders, was the architect of Truman's nomination. But
there is no real evidence of that, apart from Flynn's delightfully exaggerated autobiography, published in 1947.[5] The president's principal represen-
tatives in Chicago were Hannegan and Walker, and in any event they were
too hardened in politics to be scared by any histrionics by Flynn, who
claimed that he shouted, swore, and sufficiently carried on to get their
attention. What Flynn did was remind them that they should consult the
president. Years later Walker remembered that he, the postmaster general
and Hannegan's predecessor as national chairman, could not be for Truman unless Byrnes was out; with Byrnes still in the race such a course
would have been suicidal, dividing the conservative vote at the convention. All Wallace needed was a bare majority; after the 1936 Democratic
convention the old two-thirds rule, by which any successful candidate
needed two-thirds of the vote, had been abandoned.

Truman probably learned from Hannegan on Monday night, July 17,
that the president had chosen him. That in itself was interesting, he might
have said to himself, but not overwhelming, for the president had said
pleasant things about many people, including Wallace and Byrnes. Perhaps
it was only his turn. Also, the president had not told him personally but
only secondhand, through Hannegan.

Then the next morning, Tuesday, July 18, Truman received news of
perhaps equal importance. Breakfasting with Sidney Hillman, he heard the
latter say that Wallace was labor's first choice, but as for its second choice,
he was looking at Truman. This was remarkable news, for if the president
would keep his word, Truman could get the support of labor, and that
would put him over. Probably for the first time Truman, having loyally

gone to the convention and plumped for Byrnes, realized that he might be the candidate.

He did not quite know what to do but realized that he needed a public statement by the president. The latter's saying something in private did not count; one had to get Roosevelt out in public, or the slippery president might change his mind. And so on Wednesday afternoon, July 19, just after the convention opened, Truman was invited over to the Blackstone Hotel, where Bob Hannegan had a two-room suite. There were the party leaders, and the telephone rang; it was the president. Actually, Hannegan had put Roosevelt up to the call. The president asked if Hannegan had gotten "that fellow" lined up. The chairman said no, he was acting like a damned Missouri mule.

"Well," came the response, "tell him if he wants to break up the Democratic Party in the middle of a war that's his responsibility." With that, the president banged down the receiver.

"Now what do you say?" asked Hannegan. As Truman remembered, he said, "Jesus Christ!" He may have added, "Why the hell didn't he tell me in the first place?"

The problem with Wallace was not over, and until near the end of the convention the vice president had at least a fighting chance. He or his supporters—it is difficult to believe he was innocent in this matter—tried to stampede the convention on Thursday night, July 20, immediately after the president's acceptance speech, made by radio from San Diego. It was a near thing, in which the Wallace-ites bribed the convention organist to play the Iowa song, "Iowa, Iowa, that's where the tall corn grows!" The organist did not have a telephone on his console but had a light above one of the manuals, calling his attention to a mistaken selection, the need to change. He could not miss it if turned on, but somehow he did not manage to see it. Pauley, who was on the platform and in an apoplectic rage, told one of his assistants to get up there and cut the organ's wires with a fire ax. Mayor Kelly meanwhile declared the crowded hall, which contained thirty-five thousand people, ten thousand over its seating capacity (Wallace supporters had taken over the balconies and forced themselves onto the floor), a fire hazard. Hannegan turned to the convention's chairman, Senator Samuel D. Jackson of Indiana, and, red-faced, shouted to him to "get right up there now and I mean now" and close the meeting, "or I'll do it for you!" Jackson, a Wallace supporter, sweating, remembering perhaps that he had been told sometime before by the party chairman, Hannegan, that he, Jackson, was Hannegan's chairman "and, by God, not to forget it," did as he was told.

That was the end. The next day, July 21, Truman took the nomination on the second ballot. For the first ballot the leaders encouraged favorite sons, of whom there were a dozen, who offset Wallace's vote. Then on the second ballot, after they spoke to the state chairmen and delegates, relating what the president wanted, everything went to Truman. After the delegations changed their Wallace votes, the vice president ended up with 105 votes, and Truman received 1,031. When Iowa was called, the delegates went for Truman, with even Wallace voting for Truman.

2

Truman knew that the nomination meant the presidency, for Roosevelt would be reelected and could not possibly survive a fourth term, and when the expected happened on April 12, 1945, he took over as best he could. The extraordinary surprise of it all was that he did so well with the often novel tasks, almost overwhelming tasks, in foreign policy. Because of the defeat of Germany and Japan, a brand-new international situation confronted the new resident of 1600 Pennsylvania Avenue. Unless world affairs were to turn toward chaos it was necessary to project American power abroad on a long-term basis. Truman established the lines of projection so well that they preserved the Republic to the end of the century and beyond, after the collapse of the Soviet Union and the almost simultaneous rise of international terrorism.

At the outset of his presidency Truman had to concentrate on domestic problems. He presided over the very large task of demobilization and reconversion, if not always with as much success as he wished. Demobilization was hasty, and reconversion met with labor trouble and inflation, but Truman's measures enjoyed far more success than followed any previous American war, notably World War I. He sought to continue his predecessor's New Deal, but the American people rejected the Fair Deal. They appear either to have been preoccupied with the changes in foreign policy or to have tired of social and economic reform, at least for the moment.

It is interesting that, contrary to the president's many contemporary and later detractors, Truman did not rush into a confrontation with the Soviets but waited two years until announcement of the so-called Truman Doctrine (he was sensitive to using his name for policies, and the newspaper press gave the speech of March 1947 its Monrovian title). He knew— he discovered it from Roosevelt's advisers, Admiral William D. Leahy, Ambassador W. Averell Harriman, and others—that Roosevelt's last days had been marked by almost open disagreement with the Russians. The question was whether the differences would become permanent. The reason for delay was partly domestic, that is, preoccupation with returning the nation to peacetime pursuits. It was also the need to let the dust settle and attempt to discover what the Soviets desired.

To the reasons for going slow with the Soviet Union the president brought his study of history and, so fortunate for historians, his habit of thought that required writing down what was on his mind. He was a reader of history, not in a scholarly way, by delving into monographs and other detailed accounts, but in a less formal way, by reading popular works. He read biographies by Claude G. Bowers, Marquis James, and Douglas S. Freeman. What he took from that reading was not so much a wisdom about American history as an interest in the statements and expressions of American national purpose, which he combined with his longtime habit of letter writing (1,268 letters survived of his correspondence with his wife alone) into an almost compulsive desire to express himself on the written page. Truman wrote down what he thought, in letters but also in occasional dated accounts that amount to a diary, and in memorandums. These statements his secretary, Rose A. Conway, filed in copy or original with the result that when his papers opened at the Harry S. Truman Library in the 1970s, and the letters to his wife became available in 1983, students of his presidency were able to learn more about the chief executive's thoughts and the movement of his ideas than was possible for any of his predecessors and probably will be possible for any of his successors.

Experience in Missouri politics entered into the calculations of what to do with the Soviet Union. Truman liked to compare Stalin to the late political "boss" of Kansas City, Thomas J. Pendergast. He had been impressed by Stalin while at the Potsdam Conference, and for a while during the conference sessions (his enthusiasm wore thin toward the end) found him attractive because of his straightforwardness and terseness (the latter quality was welcome because of Prime Minister Churchill's loquacity). Stalin, Truman initially believed, was like Tom Pendergast. The boss had been brusque and terse. It was not easy to get a commitment but when he made one he kept it. Then, too, there was the way in which Truman had served as presiding judge, which meant principal county commissioner, of Jackson County, the county that contained Kansas City. Truman lived in Independence, ten miles from the center of Kansas City, and his political base was there and in the surrounding rural hinterland. He and Boss Tom virtually divided the county in terms of power, with Truman the carefully diplomatic Democratic leader in his preserve and the boss running the city. Matters worked out fairly well, with cooperation that was not merely amicable but efficient, for no time was lost in useless opposition. There was nothing Truman could do against Pendergast, whose hold on the city was so tight it seemed irreversible, perpetual, and perhaps anyway what the sinful city (Truman believed) deserved.

In observing Soviet moves during the early postwar era the president trusted that he could arrange a division of responsibilities and territory much like what he had known a decade and a half before. To an outside observer the possibility of such an arrangement might seem foolish, there being little or no carryover from American to world politics. For all Pendergast's grasping need for money during the final years of power in Kansas City, necessary because of enormous losses from betting on horse races all over the country, the boss was neither a cruel man like Stalin nor possessed of Stalin's implacable suspicions. Russia was not America—the people were brought up so differently. But this hope of a modus vivendi, as obtained in Jackson County, marked the early part of Truman's Russian policy.

When hope of compromise came to an end, the president turned from a policy of isolation with occasional intervention to full and continuous participation in European and world affairs. On March 12, 1947, Truman announced support for Greece and Turkey in what became known as the Truman Doctrine speech. Twelve weeks later, on June 5, Secretary of State Marshall during an address at the Harvard University commencement proposed a program of massive aid for the economies of Western Europe. The change in policy culminated two years later with the signing of the North Atlantic Treaty in Washington on April 4, 1949.

To some Americans at the time, and perhaps more today, the Truman Doctrine did not, and does not, read especially well. Secretary Marshall, who was in Paris when the president delivered it, did not like the text and believed it too dramatic, even provocative. The wording was laconic. The speech may have been drawn that way because of the advice of the chairman of the Senate foreign relations committee, Arthur H. Vandenberg of Michigan, who allegedly told Truman to "scare hell" out of the country, so as to obtain a congressional appropriation for Greece and Turkey.

Apart from the speech's abrupt paragraphs, another objection was that it was not specific about offering assistance, military or monetary, to any country threatened by communism. This raised the possibility that the Truman administration was offering a global doctrine, even to unworthy nations, so long as they claimed they were under pressure from the Soviet Union. In actual fact, Undersecretary of State Dean Acheson had told speechwriter Joseph Jones to pitch the speech on a worldwide level, just as Roosevelt would have done, and ask for an appropriation for Greece and Turkey. But his cautionary advice, which became known when Jones published it in 1955, did nothing to quiet Truman's critics, who for a generation, until after the Vietnam War, accused him of advancing a worldwide doctrine.[6]

The speech set the lines of policy. Americans, the historian Dexter Perkins once related, are fond of doctrines; they like grand public announcements.[7] Although presidents since Monroe have proposed doctrines, most of the pronouncements have been forgotten. But this is the way of American politics, and for that reason, and for what it meant in the resolution of an enormous foreign policy decision, Truman's doctrine can rightly take its place alongside the pronouncement of 1823. Indeed it was more important than the original doctrine, for the latter, as every reader of American history knows, required in Latin America the support of ships of the British Navy, making the United States "only a cockboat in the wake of the British man-of-war."[8] The Truman Doctrine required real national commitment.

It may be too much to credit President Truman with the other cold war policies of his administration, those that followed during the next two years: the Marshall Plan, the Berlin airlift of 1948–1949, and the North Atlantic Treaty—or so the president's critics at the time and later have said. It is true that the Marshall Plan was a national program, not the president's personal program. The president named it for his secretary of state because he needed Marshall's name to get it through the Republican

Eightieth Congress and because he admired Marshall above all other public figures he had known. Beyond consenting to the program and presiding over it, Truman had little to do with the $13.3 billion given mostly to western Europe in 1948–1951. A scholarly authority on the plan, Michael J. Hogan, has gone so far as to say that the plan did not really revive the Continent's economies, that Europeans themselves furnished most of the funds necessary to create a postwar economic infrastructure.[9] Still, behind the Marshall Plan was the Truman Doctrine, the new base of American foreign policy, introduced to Congress by President Truman.

The Berlin airlift was not Truman's creation but a momentary reaction to the Russian blockade, one instituted by the military governor of the American zone of Germany, General Lucius D. Clay. When Clay proposed it to his air force commander, General Curtis E. LeMay, the latter was astonished, hardly believing it possible. Clay had little faith in it and, snapping his fingers, told a German reporter he would not give that much for it. Truman announced the airlift a day after Clay announced it.

But the above is a simple statement of what happened, and Truman had much more to do with the airlift than was known at the time. Within the administration that summer of 1948, when the airlift was promising no more than a stopgap, administration figures—that is, cabinet officers and the leading military figures in Washington—oscillated in their judgments over what should be done about the Russian blockade of Germany's former capital city. One group wished a showdown, in which the U.S. Army in the American zone of Germany would send an armored train through the Soviet zone, to Berlin, and force a response that might lead to war. Another group wanted to do nothing, to give in to Russian pressure and discontinue all effort to supply the two million residents of Berlin with food and coal via an airlift. This might have meant that Western forces, American, British, and French, would have had to leave Berlin, abandon the city, allow it to pass under Russian control. Truman refused either of these alternatives and opted to continue the airlift—which turned out to be a technical triumph that persuaded the Soviets to end the blockade. Truman's was the decisive voice in this course.

In the instance of the North Atlantic Treaty and its military and political result, the organization known as NATO, it could be argued that Truman was not its author. The British foreign secretary, Ernest Bevin, suggested it to Marshall during a London conference of foreign ministers late in 1947. Throughout 1948, Truman was seeking election to the presidency in a contest that no one other than the president, not even Mrs. Truman, believed he could win. But during that year of campaigning he supported Marshall, who was pursuing Bevin's suggestion. Discussions over NATO went on, month after month. It was a brave thing for the president to have done. If the discussions had become known they would have hurt his chances in a tight race, persuading considerable numbers of Democratic voters that Republican criticisms of Truman's foreign policy were correct. He supported Marshall and shared his belief that it was not possible to announce a doctrine and an economic plan without, sooner or later, establishing a European defense force that could remove or at least balance the nearby Soviet forces.

After the election it became possible to create NATO, and with inclusion of many more nations than Bevin had anticipated. The new treaty was not a European enlargement of the Treaty of Dunkirk of 1947, which was only between Britain and France; or even of the Brussels Pact of the next year, which included the Benelux countries, Belgium, the Netherlands, and Luxembourg; or even a so-called dumbbell arrangement of two treaties, between the Europeans on the one side and Britain and Canada and the United States on the other. It was a grand arrangement of twelve nations that, with the later inclusion of Greece, Turkey, West Germany, and Spain, lasted beyond the collapse of the Soviet Union.

The testing of the nation's new foreign policy came during the Korean War, when President Truman showed a steely unwillingness to "cut and run," in particular after the Chinese intervention in November 1950, which for several unnerving weeks threatened a debacle to United Nations forces (which were almost entirely American). The Americans had withdrawn occupation troops from South Korea and prudently refused to give President Syngman Rhee the planes and tanks he almost certainly would have taken into North Korea (as late as 1954 Rhee, in a visit to the White House, proposed a preventive war). The joint chiefs of staff desired to avoid protecting South Korea, which they said was militarily indefensible save by American forces that were unavailable. The commander in Japan, General MacArthur, saw no reason to protect South Korea. Secretary of State Marshall's successor, Acheson, announced that Korea was outside the U.S. defense perimeter. The dictator of North Korea, Kim Il Sung, seeing this writing on the wall, assured Stalin that the Americans would not intervene, and Stalin agreed, giving his consent to the North Korean attack on South Korea, removing Russian military advisers to the North Korean army just before the Russian-designed and Russian-supplied attack. Truman intervened because he had to, otherwise Japan would have been militarily at the mercy of the North Koreans and behind them the Soviet Union. It also appeared as if the invasion was an attempt by the Soviets to divert American troops to a corner of East Asia and then attack the NATO allies in Western Europe. This threat required sending four more divisions to NATO to supplement the two then present, in addition to the six sent to Korea. All in all the Korean War showed that Stalin had turned hostile with a vengeance. Truman was absolutely right in opposing Stalin in Korea. After U.S. intervention not merely saved South Korea but threatened to take North Korea, Stalin pleaded with Mao Tse-tung to intervene. When the Chinese intervention turned to stalemate Stalin advised the Chinese to continue the war so as to wear the Americans down, which they did until the Russian dictator died in March 1953. They agreed, through the North Koreans, to an armistice the following July.

In establishing American foreign policy President Truman was forced to make decisions about nuclear weapons. During the war against Japan no decision he made was subject to such prolonged and adverse criticism as the decision on July 24, 1945, while at the Potsdam Conference, to give permission to the Twentieth Air Force to drop nuclear weapons after he had left the conference on August 2. Suffice to say that by this time the interception and decoding of Japanese radio messages, a secret operation for both Europe and Asia known as Ultra, was showing a rapid buildup of troops and planes on the southernmost Japanese home island of Kyushu.[10] Behind Truman's later explanation of fear of half a million or a million casualties resulting from an invasion there and from planned attacks on Honshu and the Tokyo plain was the very real possibility that the fears were justified. For this reason he made the decision to end the war as quickly as possible, if necessary by the weapons he had at his disposal.

The subsequent decisions of his administration in regard to nuclear weapons were, each of them, very difficult, although not of the order of the Japanese bombings. When it came to proposing nuclear limitation or disarmament, he resorted to the so-called Acheson-Lilienthal plan of 1946 for international control of nuclear weapons. It failed in the United Nations partly because Bernard Baruch, who presented the plan named for the then undersecretary of state and the chairman of the Atomic Energy Commission, David E. Lilienthal, chose to add a proposal of enforcement. The latter was unnecessary because the United States was the only nation strong enough to try to enforce any UN resolution against Russian misbehavior. The Soviet representative in the United Nations chose to be offended by the idea of enforcement. The subject of nuclear weapons came up again in 1948 at the time of the Berlin blockade, when the armed services, desiring physical control of the nuclear arsenal so as to be prepared in the event of an emergency, raised the issue of custody. Truman was against removing the weapons from control of the civilian Atomic Energy Commission and said so several times. The Korean War weakened his resolve, and he allowed nonnuclear components to go into storage bins on Guam. Because most of the nuclear arsenal was to be used against the Soviet Union, he permitted components to be loaded aboard aircraft carriers in the Atlantic or Mediterranean and later stored in facilities in Newfoundland and Britain. In January 1953, just before leaving office, he approved transfer of completed weapons assemblies to the military.

The decision to produce a hydrogen bomb, made in January 1950, came after a seven-minute discussion with Acheson, Secretary of Defense Louis Johnson, and AEC Chairman Lilienthal. Truman approved production in order to stay ahead of the Russians and to have a bargaining chip, if necessary. There is some reason to believe that he possessed information on the treasonous behavior of a British scientist, Klaus Fuchs, who had taken part in the wartime Anglo-American program to produce nuclear weapons and in postwar discussion of a hydrogen bomb. Fuchs's knowledge of hydrogen-bomb technology, it turned out, was of a process that would not work, but he did pass to his Soviet handlers the design of the nuclear weapon exploded over Nagasaki, the second of the nuclear bombings of Japan in 1945. This design the Russians employed to detonate their first nuclear explosion a year before the president decided to seek production of a hydrogen bomb.

In regard to the nation's much-vaunted nuclear arsenal beginning in 1945, there are some calculations that cannot be proved until the opening of American and Soviet records but that are intriguing in their possibilities. Throughout 1947, when Truman was announcing a new foreign policy, it appears as if the United States possessed virtually no nuclear weapons because the AEC, having taken over the army's Manhattan District nuclear organization on January 1, had no bomb-assembly teams until December of that year. To ready a single bomb required a team of twenty-four men and nearly two days. Because of the need to recharge a weapon's batteries, the bomb could not remain in a plane ready for dropping for more than forty-eight hours. Moreover, a vital part of the bomb, the polonium initiator necessary to ready a critical mass, had a half-life of 138 days, and initiators were in short supply in 1947. The nation's nuclear defenselessness may have been even worse than problems connected with the lack of bomb-assembly teams and polonium initiators. When Fuchs confessed to espionage in 1950, it became evident that he might have compromised the radar-fusing mechanism of the Nagasaki-type plutonium (Fat Boy) bomb, which until 1948 was the only type of bomb in the U.S. arsenal. If he had compromised the mechanism, the Soviets might have jammed the bombs' radars, making these weapons impossible to aim. In any event, until about the time of the Korean War, and whatever the nature of the nuclear arsenal, the Strategic Air Command was unable to drop bombs anywhere near targets; in a simulated bomb run over Dayton in 1949, not a single SAC plane "hit" the target.[11]

Despite difficulties during the eventful and danger-ridden years of his presidency, Truman kept his attention on his principal task, which was to exert American national power in Europe and East Asia in ways that would contain the Soviet Union and maintain world peace. In large part—the Korean War excepted—he managed the task. It was a great achievement. By the end of his years in the White House, the basic policies of change were in effect: the Truman Doctrine, the Marshall Plan, and NATO. The country's weak conventional military forces after demobilization were greatly bolstered by the mobilization during the Korean War, when military budgets were three times their size in 1945–1950. Nuclear forces and the means to deliver them also had turned around, with Mark IV mass-produced bombs replacing the possibly vulnerable Mark IIIs (Nagasaki plutonium) and with the Strategic Air Command at last a highly efficient arm of delivery. During this time President Truman often lacked popular support, for after a honeymoon between his appearance in the presidency in April 1945 and the end of the Pacific War in August, his poll ratings began to go down. They moved up after his victory in the presidential election in 1948 and during the first weeks of the Korean War. Thereafter they dropped precipitately, and in early 1951 a Gallup poll revealed an approval rating of 23 percent, as compared with Richard M. Nixon's 24 percent approval in 1974 on the eve of impeachment. But the president refused to change course. He believed there could be no turning back and that the American people in the long run would see that. Such steadfastness, in addition to the extraordinary measures that he took in foreign policy in the crucial years 1945–1953, should confer greatness upon the man for whom President Roosevelt without much thought arranged the vice presidential nomination at the now-forgotten convention in Chicago in 1944.

$\mathcal{N}otes$

One. Who Are These People?

Originally published in *Presidential Studies Quarterly* 32 (December 2002): 664–71.

1. The historian Charles Seymour edited House's papers and arranged for their deposit at Yale University. For many years the diary was inaccessible. Eventually opened, it is now available on microfilm. Shortly before his death in 1938, House spoke at length to Seymour about what he considered the malign influence of the second Mrs. Wilson—of how he, House, had sought to get the president to compromise over the treaty's first twenty-six articles that constituted the Covenant of the League of Nations, and how Mrs. Wilson advised her husband against anything House proposed, describing him to her husband as "Colonel Mouse." Just before Seymour himself died in 1963, he related what House had told him (Charles Seymour, "End of a Friendship?").

2. Boone dictated his memoir, and this may explain its literary infelicities, veering from careful analysis to banal description. Available in the manuscript division of the Library of Congress, it is much worth consulting. For Boone, see the excellent work by Milton F. Heller Jr., *The Presidents' Doctor: An Insider's View of Three First Families.* Carl S. Anthony's *Florence Harding: The First Lady, the Jazz Age, and the Death of America's Most Scandalous President* is nominally a biography of the president's wife but is in fact an attack on the president; it contains dozens of pages of notes, giving the appearance of scholarship, but is full of hearsay and innuendo.

3. See Mark Sullivan, *Our Times: The Twenties;* Frederick Lewis Allen, *Only Yesterday: An Informal History of the Nineteen-Twenties;* William Allen White, *Masks in a Pageant;* Alice Roosevelt Longworth, *Crowded Hours: Reminiscences of Alice Roosevelt Longworth.*

4. Hoover's *Memoirs* were written years before publication, and their author did not revise when presumably new insights and the memoirs of associates and

political opponents, not to mention articles and books by scholars, might have changed his judgments. *The Autobiography of Calvin Coolidge,* like President Hoover's memoirs, is very much the composition of its author. It includes typically aphoristic commentaries and has its didactic passages, but it is worth attention because of its openness. Coolidge was no man to spill his thoughts, but insofar as he believed a statement useful—to the nation, not to himself (he was a selfless person)—he set out his views. The president died in January 1933, before the Franklin D. Roosevelt administration, and admitted to a friendly newspaperman, not long before he passed on, that he did not fit the times. It has been customary to make fun of the *Autobiography.* It is, again, worth attention.

5. A notable example of a political appointment to the Court occurred in 1946, when the death of Harlan F. Stone, then the chief justice, a Coolidge appointee as associate justice, and previously dean of the Columbia University Law School, gave Jackson the opportunity he foreclosed. There followed the choice of a Kentucky politician, Fred M. Vinson. The latter's task, according to President Harry S. Truman, was to halt the disagreements on the Court, typified by the contention between Jackson and Black.

6. For the conspiracy to substitute Senator Truman for Vice President Wallace, see my *Choosing Truman: The Democratic Convention of 1944.*

7. For Potter's article, see "Sketches for the Roosevelt Portrait."

8. The president died in 1972, and beginning in 1977 the Truman Library archivists opened 340 Hollinger boxes (each five inches wide, with the papers inside stacked vertically) of the private papers, including two boxes in the president's handwriting—which I by chance saw in December 1978 and thereby realized the importance of the papers (*Off the Record: The Private Papers of Harry S. Truman*). Robert H. Ferrell, ed., *Dear Bess: The Letters from Harry to Bess Truman, 1910–1959,* is a selection from 1,268 letters opened in 1983, all except one in Truman's hand (he believed that a letter was not personal unless handwritten). Robert J. Donovan, in *Conflict and Crisis: The Presidency of Harry S. Truman, 1945–1948* and *Tumultuous Years: The Presidency of Harry S. Truman, 1949–1953,* used the private papers but not extensively; at the time Donovan's books appeared, the *Dear Bess* letters were unavailable. Monte M. Poen, ed., *Strictly Personal and Confidential: The Letters Harry Truman Never Mailed,* is vastly amusing as well as instructive of presidential opinions. The journalist Merle Miller celebrated the president's openness with a popular compilation published in 1974, *Plain Speaking: An Oral Biography of Harry S. Truman.* Historians and political scientists adopted it for classroom use, and the book remains in print. Unfortunately, it is a hoax; see Francis Heller and Robert H. Ferrell, "Plain Faking."

Two. Woodrow Wilson: A Misfit in Office

Originally published in Joseph G. Dawson III, ed., *Commanders in Chief: Presidential Leadership in Modern Wars,* 65–86, 194–98. Reprinted with permission.

1. A reader perhaps needs warning that my point of view agrees with that of some students and differs from that of others. See, for instance, Edward M. Coffman, *The War to End All Wars: The American Military Experience in World War I,* who writes that "since Woodrow Wilson had little interest in military matters, his secretary of war assumed great responsibilities in the spring of 1917" (20). Harvey A. DeWeerd, *President Wilson Fights His War: World War I and the American Intervention,* concludes, "Wilson was able to go through a year and a half of war without ever acting as 'Commander-in-Chief'" (251). Ernest R. May, ed., *The Ultimate Decision: The President as Commander in Chief,* relates how Wilson "evaded his duty as commander in chief in order to do his larger duty as President of the United States" (131). A significant, contrasting, pro-Wilson viewpoint is provided by David F. Trask, "Woodrow Wilson and the Reconciliation of Force and Diplomacy, 1917–1918." See also the excellent analysis by Betty Miller Unterberger, *The United States, Revolutionary Russia, and the Rise of Czechoslovakia,* which agrees with Trask. Unterberger sees a large role for Wilson in dealing with the military demand to declare war against Austria-Hungary after the defeat of the Italian Army at Caporetto in 1917, in his relationship with the Supreme War Council, in his decisions in regard to the eastern front (sending American troops to Murmansk and Vladivostok), in the support of his generals in winning the war on the western front, and in his interest in problems involved with modern and coalition warfare—especially when the United States in April 1917 declared war only against Germany and not against all the Central Powers. It may be, of course, that the "sides" in this academic disagreement are attempting to deal with different things. My side considers the phrase *commander in chief* in a more narrowly military sense than does the other. For general works on the United States at war see Grosvenor B. Clarkson, *Industrial America in the World War: The Strategy behind the Line, 1917–1918;* Bernard M. Baruch, *American Industry in the War;* David F. Trask, *The United States in the Supreme War Council: American War Aims and Inter-Allied Strategy, 1917–1918;* Daniel R. Beaver, *Newton D. Baker and the American War Effort, 1917–1918;* and Robert D. Cuff, *The War Industries Board: Business Government Relations during World War I.* It is perhaps worth mentioning that Wilson's Democratic successor, Franklin D. Roosevelt, was highly critical of his administration. Making allowance for what might have been casual overstatement, it is interesting that FDR told Secretary of the Interior Harold L. Ickes that "Wilson literally didn't know what was going on in the Government." FDR said that Wilson left everything to the chairman of the War Industries Board, Bernard Baruch; his secretary of the treasury, William G. McAdoo; "and a few others." And again: "The President said that there were two kinds of Presidents, one like himself who kept track of everything and the other like Woodrow Wilson, who did not know what was going on but who let his Cabinet run the show." See *The Secret Diary of Harold L. Ickes: The Lowering Clouds, 1939–1941,* 201, 232.

2. Arthur S. Link, *Wilson: The Road to the White House,* 2.

3: Here my learned colleague Betty Unterberger disagrees. Wilson, she writes (letter, June 4, 1990), "grasped the true nature of modern war more quickly than did most Americans." He sensed the horrors of modern technological warfare and certainly understood the relevance of modern technology in war much more clearly than did his great contemporary, Theodore Roosevelt. See John Milton Cooper Jr., *The Warrior and the Priest: Woodrow Wilson and Theodore Roosevelt,* 310, 325–26, and Arthur S. Link et al., eds., *The Papers of Woodrow Wilson,* vol. 40 (1982): 69–70; Donald E. Davis and Eugene P. Trani, *The First Cold War: The Legacy of Woodrow Wilson in U.S.-Soviet Relations.*

4. Robert H. Ferrell, *Woodrow Wilson and World War I, 1917–1921,* 103–4.

5. In the 1930s, President Roosevelt appointed Denman a federal appeals judge, and he held that post until his death, long after his moment in the limelight.

6. Goethals seems to have learned of Denman's description of him as an SOB and got up a magnanimous letter of resignation, which George Rublee took to the president's private secretary, Joseph P. Tumulty. Rublee's oral history, 155–56.

7. Ferrell, *Woodrow Wilson and World War I,* 102.

8. Alfred D. Chandler Jr. and Stephen Salsbury, *Pierre S. Du Pont and the Making of the Modern Corporation,* 359–430.

9. There was a side of Baker, not often seen, that was cold and hard. Bishop Charles H. Brent, a leader in the Episcopal Church who spent time in France supervising the chaplains of the AEF and who talked to Baker about chaplains, found him not merely ignorant but also resistant. When the secretary told the bishop that the latter should feel free to write him personally about the chaplain problem, Brent told his diary he assuredly would not, that Baker was too cold a fish for such an exchange, and that the secretary thought the war would be won by force and politics (Brent diary, September 23, 1918, Brent papers, Library of Congress).

10. Frederick Palmer, *Newton D. Baker: America at War,* 1:11.

11. Ibid., 1:159.

12. Coffman, *The War to End All Wars,* 21.

13. Elting E. Morison, "Newton D. Baker."

14. C. H. Cramer, *Newton D. Baker: A Biography,* 138. See also Beaver, *Baker and the American War Effort.*

15. House diary, March 27, 1917, House papers, Yale University.

16. Baker to James G. Harbord, December 30, 1929, Harbord papers, Library of Congress.

17. Stanley Washburn oral history, 112–13; Franklin K. Lane to George W. Lane, February 16, 1917, in Anne W. Lane and Louise H. Wall, eds., *The Letters of Franklin K. Lane: Personal and Political,* 238.

18. For Scott and the Indians see Angie Debo, *A History of the Indians of the United States,* 237.

19. Mrs. Hugh Scott to Baker, May 27, 1918, Baker papers, Library of Congress.

20. The influence of Bliss on the Peace Conference is not easy to measure, and it may well be that the general was of considerable importance. President Wilson praised Bliss, for which see Arthur S. Link et al., eds., *The Papers of Woodrow Wilson*, vol. 53 (1986): 320 ("he considered him a real statesman, all of his judgments being mature"); vol. 54 (1986): 34 (the president "spoke of Bliss in the highest terms"). See also the books by David F. Trask: *The United States in the Supreme War Council* and *General Tasker Howard Bliss and the "Sessions of the World," 1919*. When the president nominated Bliss as a peace commissioner, Colonel House thought well of the choice: "General Bliss is the best appointment, Lansing and White [Secretary of State Robert Lansing and the retired diplomat Henry White] are weak and will be of but little help" (House diary, December 1, 1918, House papers). But opinions changed. During the conference Charles Seymour wrote his wife, "I finally take back what I said some months ago about Bliss. He is a man of very interesting ideas and I think in the main very good ones. But he lacks the force to put them over, or perhaps I should say the peculiar power of influencing the President; and the President is all powerful. The General also lacks the power of organization. Hence his influence here has been practically negligible" (Harold B. Whiteman, ed., *Charles Seymour: Letters from the Paris Peace Conference*, 207). The journalist Stephen Bonsal assisted House at the conference and wrote in an undated portion of his diary for August 1919, "Bliss, of course, was a great mistake. . . . Bliss was constantly making amateurish political suggestions which so bored the President that he could hardly bring himself to listen to Bliss when he spoke on matters within his competence." In an entry for September 19, Bonsal credited the general with remarking about the president: "I do not like the man and I have no confidence in him. There is something feminine, feline, cattish, about him which I abhor." Wilson himself had said of Bliss, in Bonsal's hearing: "I sent Bliss over here to advise me on military problems, but whenever he opens his mouth he talks to me about the Jugo-Slavs—of whom he has but a superficial knowledge, if any." The above diary is in the Bonsal papers, Library of Congress.

21. Letter of December 24, 1917, microfilm, Bryce papers, Bodleian Library, Oxford University. Lord Bryce formerly served as Great Britain's ambassador to the United States.

22. Memorandum by Colonel J. S. Fair, April 1, 1919, Fair papers, National Archives; James E. Hewes, *From Root to McNamara: Army Organization and Administration, 1900–1963*.

23. House diary, December 18, 1917, January 18, 1918, House papers. Ferrell, *Woodrow Wilson and World War I*, 105.

24. The colonel's diary for January 17, 1918, deserves quotation in extenso (House papers):

> Last night when Garfield's coal order was given out, bedlam broke loose. Press associations, newspaper editors etc., etc. made my life miserable. This has continued all day. There is nothing that the administration has

done that I regret so much. It may be necessary, but it certainly was not necessary to do it in such a casual and abrupt way. It is one of the things I have feared the President would sometime do. He seems to have done it. I have never heard such a storm of protest. What I am afraid of is that it will weaken confidence in his administrative ability and bring Congress about his ears. I look to see an insistent demand that some change be made in the organization responsible for the conduct of the war. This question has disturbed me since my return from Europe. Men of every shade of political opinion condemn the organization as it now exists. The President and Secretary Baker seem to be the only ones that think the organization is as it should be. Men like [Robert S.] Lovett, Nelson Perkins, Baruch, Cyrus McCormick, Bainbridge Colby and other staunch supporters of the Administration have but one story to tell. They look to me to influence the President. I have hesitated to mention the matter to him for the reason that I tried at the beginning of the war to get him to accept what I thought to be the right sort of organiza-tion—an organization which everybody now thinks is essential. I do not like to intrude my advice upon him again. He knows quite well what I think, and he knows that I do not believe that he has an effective war organization, and I have been content to let it go at that. The fact that he does not consult me about these matters indicates that he knows we disagree, but he had believed he could work it out along the lines which he has pursued. However, matters have gotten so bad now since this coal order of Garfield's that I have concluded, in justice to the Presi-dent, that I should give a helping hand whether he asks for it or not. I have therefore arranged for Secretary Baker to come over Sunday to be with me a large part of the day. If I can get him into a proper frame of mind to see the necessity for a radical and thorough reorganization of affairs, I will take it up with the President. The President will not want it but, at the moment, it looks as if he will have no choice, for if he does not do it himself, Congress may force it upon him.

25. Reed Smoot diary, January 29, 1918, courtesy Jan Shipps; Colville Bar-clay to Arthur Balfour, January 30, Balfour papers, Public Record Office; David Lawrence to Wilson, January 28, Baker papers.

26. Quoted in Arthur S. Link, *Woodrow Wilson: A Brief Biography*, 23.

27. See Edward M. Coffman, *The Hilt of the Sword: The Career of Peyton C. March*.

Three. Warren G. Harding's Reputation

Originally published in Robert H. Ferrell, *The Strange Deaths of President Hard-ing*, 134–65, 183–86.

1. Clinton W. Gilbert, *Behind the Mirrors: The Psychology of Disintegration at Washington,* iv.

2. Clinton W. Gilbert, *The Mirrors of Washington,* 3–4.

3. Gilbert, *Behind the Mirrors,* 35.

4. Ibid., 6.

5. Ibid., 102; Gilbert, *Mirrors of Washington,* 12–13.

6. Gilbert, *Behind the Mirrors,* 6.

7. Henry L. Mencken, *Baltimore Sun,* September 9, 1921, in Malcolm Moos, ed., *A Carnival of Buncombe,* 4–5.

8. Ibid.

9. Ibid., 8 (February 9, 1920); 16 (July 26, 1920); 25 (October 4, 1920).

10. Ibid., 19.

11. Ibid., 31 (October 18, 1920).

12. Ibid., 28.

13. Ibid., 15.

14. Ibid., 22–23 (October 4, 1920).

15. Ibid., 32.

16. Ibid., 20 (September 13, 1920); 38–40 (March 7, 1921).

17. Ibid., 20 (September 13, 1920).

18. Ibid., 26 (October 4, 1920).

19. For the *American Mercury,* I am indebted to Randolph C. Downes's unpublished "The Harding Muckfest"; Downes analyzed each issue for 1924.

20. Moos, ed., *Carnival,* xvi–xvii.

21. Letter of March 31, 1962, folder 15, box 6, Downes papers, University of Toledo.

22. William Allen White, *Autobiography,* 587.

23. Randolph C. Downes, "The Harding Papers," 5, address to the Society of American Archivists, April 28, 1966, in Cincinnati. Copy in the Downes papers.

24. William Allen White, *Masks in a Pageant,* 425, 433–34.

25. Ibid., 432.

26. Ibid., 424–30.

27. Andrew Sinclair, *The Available Man: The Life behind the Masks of Warren Gamaliel Harding,* 297.

28. He would have liked to have written more than the Harding chapter in *Masks,* and the year after the book appeared he was either considering a book entirely on Harding or recommending the project to a friend. "What about Harding? There's a beautiful story. . . . No one less than Voltaire or Carlyle should do it. Yet for five years my poor typewriter has had a deep dirty suppressed desire to click it out" (letter to Allan Nevins, July 27, 1929, copy in "Harding 1926–1933," box 21, Dean Albertson papers, University of Massachusetts).

29. Robert K. Murray, *The Harding Era: Warren G. Harding and His Administration,* 519–20.

30. Allan Nevins, "Warren G. Harding."

31. Alice Roosevelt Longworth, *Crowded Hours,* 324–25; Murray, *Harding Era,* 521.

32. When Alice Longworth's husband was running for the majority leadership of the House his brother-in-law recorded that his drinking was hurting his race: "I am afraid you can't teach an old dog new tricks. Nick has been a hard drinker for years so I don't think you can change him" (Theodore Roosevelt Jr. diary, May 28, 1923, box 1, Roosevelt papers, Library of Congress).

33. Letter of March 31, 1962, folder 15, box 6, Downes papers.

34. Because of his Republican contacts, Sullivan picked up gossip of interesting sorts. The story concerned a Mrs. Cross, about whom he learned from President Wilson's erstwhile private secretary, Tumulty. Reportedly, the woman had been a Harding intimate, and according to Tumulty the then senator once suffered a heart attack walking up the stairs of her apartment. Mrs. Cross sought to profit from the association, and the Wilson administration in the person of Attorney General A. Mitchell Palmer arranged for her to leave Washington. During the Harding administration Attorney General Harry M. Daugherty embarrassed the Democratic Party by moving against certain Democratic figures, including Palmer. The lawyer Frank J. Hogan was involved in some way; he was attorney for Doheny, and the involvement might have been the imminence of Senate hearings over Teapot Dome. Hogan saw the president, mentioned Democratic behavior over the Mrs. Cross affair, and Harding immediately called off Daugherty (Sullivan diary, August 2, 1923, Herbert Hoover Library).

After listening to this story, Sullivan asked Tumulty about Mrs. Mary Peck, a woman with whom President Wilson had been linked by gossip. Many years later, on October 2, 1964, a onetime reporter for the *Washington Post,* Vylla Poe Wilson, spoke with historian Dean Albertson and identified the Harding friend as Grace Cross, a "tall, beautiful blonde—exceptionally beautiful," who worked in Harding's Senate office. Vylla Wilson told of Harding letters in the possession of Mrs. Cross, which a mutual friend, Bertha Martin, literally snatched from Mrs. Cross during a luncheon on March 4, 1921, and then a week later Bertha Martin became society editor of the *Post,* through arrangement made by President Harding's friend Jess Smith ("Vylla Poe Wilson," box 24, Albertson papers). But then Vylla Wilson told Albertson that the White House chief usher, Irwin H. (Ike) Hoover, the president's alleged friend, told her he had seen Nan Britton several times leave the White House after visiting the president and that during an outing for the women of the press corps on the presidential yacht *Mayflower* Ms. Britton appeared and the captain escorted her off the ship.

35. Murray, *Harding Era,* 457–58; Sullivan diary, November 18, 1923.

36. Mark Sullivan, *Our Times: The Twenties,* 356 n, 364 n. On the second page, in a note following the first, Sullivan took back the accusation of murder.

37. Ibid., 244. *The Oxford English Dictionary* cites *normalcy* in a mathematical dictionary of 1857.

38. Samuel Hopkins Adams, *Incredible Era: The Life and Times of Warren Gamaliel Harding*, 80.

39. Ibid., 155; Murray, *Harding Era*, 523.

40. Greenslet to Daugherty, October 18, 1939, copy in "Harding—1939–1962," box 21, Albertson papers.

41. Wolff to Boone, January 10, 1963, "Harding," box 29, Boone papers, Library of Congress. Boone excerpted the following line from Alice Longworth's book, "He was just a slob," as well as the passage that "He had discovered what was going on around him, and that knowledge, the worry, the thought of the disclosures and shame that were bound to come, undoubtedly undermined his health—one might say actually killed him" (*Crowded Hours*, 325). Beside these quotations he penciled question marks and "Do not believe this so." In response to Wolff's letter he wrote, "If the distortions as I recognize them in Mr. Adams' book, wherein he mentions my name, are indicative of the lack of factuality of other portions of his book, *Incredible Era*, I would be compelled to discount many of the references to other people and events to be found in his book." And again, "Too many so-called historians' writings . . . are based on hearsay and without personal knowledge of the period or people about whom they write" (Boone to Wolff, February 20, 1963, "Harding," box 29).

42. Kenneth W. Duckett, "The Harding Papers: How Some Were Burned . . ."

43. Nan Britton, *The President's Daughter*, 102, 351; White, *Masks*, 409, 413; Gaston B. Means, *The Strange Death of President Harding: From the Diaries of Gaston B. Means, a Department of Justice Investigator*, 56–57; Adams, *Incredible Era*, 101.

44. *Cleveland Plain Dealer*, July 31, 1964, folder 90, box 5, Downes papers.

45. Randolph C. Downes, "The Harding Papers," 15, Downes papers.

46. Francis Russell, *The Shadow of Blooming Grove: Warren G. Harding and His Times*, 165–68; *Columbus Citizen Journal Dispatch*, January 20, 1972, folder 90, box 5, Downes papers.

47. *Columbus Citizen Journal Dispatch*, January 20, 1972.

48. William Estabrook Chancellor, *Warren Gamaliel Harding: President of the United States*, 109. Chancellor wrote that former governor Myron T. Herrick made the offer of the trip to Japan, together with the cash payment and monthly income. The Herrick papers in the Western Reserve Historical Society, Cleveland, offer nothing on this subject. Indeed, the formality of a letter from Herrick to Harding congratulating him on his nomination for the presidency makes the possibility unlikely. In folder 148, roll 3, are undated memorandums and notes of private remarks and conversations in 1928–1929 when Herrick was ambassador to France (Herrick died in the latter year); a friend wrote them down. He told amusing stories and once asked his friend what was the similarity between the daughter of Alice and Nick Longworth, born in the mid-1920s, and a new golf ball. (Answer: "Neither has a nick in it.") The stories and remarks did not

mention Mrs. Phillips. Herrick was in France and England during most of the summer of 1920.

49. The interview appeared in the issue of July 18, 1964.

50. A reporter published an interview with Ms. Britton some months later in which the author of *The President's Daughter* spoke kindly of Mrs. Phillips and her daughter, Isabelle, with whom she had gone to school. She said the Phillipses were neighbors, that she possessed a photograph of Isabelle's pet bulldog, and she wished she would have an opportunity to see Isabelle and sit down and have a long visit. The interviewer did not mention to her the references to Mrs. Arnold in the book but quoted them extensively in the resultant article (Jane Schermerhorn, "The Love Affair That Never Died: Exclusive Interview with Nan Britton"). The reporter wrote the biographer Francis Russell, who evidently inquired, that the interview was difficult. "She didn't talk much but I think she was rather stung by the Phillips love letters and there was something like defiance in her manner when she blurted, 'Indeed I have Harding papers and they are safe—under lock and key—in a bank.' A second visit to her was prevented by her attorney" (letter of March 1, 1965, Russell papers, University of Wyoming).

51. Sinclair was irritable on that point and published an essay in the *New York Times Book Review* castigating his fellow biographers who criticized him, remarking that it was possible to obtain enough Xerox copies of the Harding papers in six days to equal six months of research in the pre-Xerox era. He also was thankful for Xerox because he detested Columbus, Ohio. In his essay he wrote that Columbus doubtless was "bonny" (he was a Scotsman) to the Columbians, "but I feel rather pre-Columbian toward the civilization which has conquered there.... I got my material and got out of town. By August I'd written up my gleanings into the first draft." It was necessary to return to Columbus to check notes, and this involved going into the Ohio Historical Society's search room, the lions' den, where the hostile biographers worked. In accord with Nathaniel Hawthorne's "Purloined Letter" he left his manuscript in full view, so no one would see it. When he submitted it to his publisher, one of the biographers wrote the editor of the series in which it was to appear, advising of the little time Sinclair spent in Columbus. The editor previously had approved the manuscript, but withdrew his approval. Fortunately, the Macmillan house editor refused to be frightened. "It no longer puzzles me," Sinclair concluded, "that some historians have become Presidents; if you finagle your way in the first profession, the second is a joy ride" (Andrew Sinclair, "The Dear Departed"). The only historian to become president was Woodrow Wilson. For a short time John Quincy Adams held the title of Boylston Professor of Rhetoric at Harvard University.

52. Sinclair, *Available Man,* 44, 277–78, 297–98.

53. Ibid., 284, 286, 295, 324.

54. Ibid., 99, 274–77.

55. Ibid., 293.

56. Francis Russell, "The Four Mysteries of Warren Harding."

57. Ibid., 83.

58. Russell, *Shadow of Blooming Grove,* 161.

59. Having made his agreement with Kefauver, Downes should have remained quiet about it, but revealed his anger to a reporter. *Dayton Journal Herald,* February 1, 1971, folder 89, box 5, Downes papers.

60. The best source for the first five polls is Robert K. Murray and Tim H. Blessing's *Greatness in the White House: Rating the Presidents, Washington through Carter,* 6–9, 16–17. For the William Ridings Jr. and Stuart B. McIver poll, see their "1990's Presidential Poll"; the Neal poll is in the *Chicago Sun-Times,* November 19, 1995.

Four. Calvin Coolidge, the Man and the President

Originally published in John Earl Haynes, ed., *Calvin Coolidge and the Coolidge Era: Essays on the History of the 1920s,* 132–48.

1. William Allen White, *Calvin Coolidge: The Man Who Is President,* 114.

2. Alfred P. Dennis, *Gods and Little Fishes,* 169–70.

3. Claude M. Fuess, *Calvin Coolidge: The Man from Vermont,* 470.

4. Boone memoir, 505, box 46, Boone papers, Library of Congress.

5. Ibid., 110.

6. Ibid., 503.

7. Fuess, *Calvin Coolidge,* 323.

8. William R. Castle Jr. to Alanson B. Houghton, December 7, 1925, box 3, Castle papers, Herbert Hoover Library.

9. Dennis, *Gods and Little Fishes,* 25.

10. Castle diary, December 2, 1927, Castle papers.

11. Boone memoir, 183.

12. Ibid., 66.

13. Ibid., 459–63.

14. Ibid., 727–28.

15. Ibid., 849.

16. Sullivan diary, December 21, 1923, Herbert Hoover Library.

17. Boone memoir, 49.

18. Ibid., 468.

19. Ibid., 50–51.

20. Ibid., 318.

21. Gilbert C. Fite, *Peter Norbeck: Prairie Statesman,* 114.

22. George Wharton Pepper, *Philadelphia Lawyer: An Autobiography,* 202.

23. Fite, *Peter Norbeck,* 114.

24. Sullivan diary, September 19, 1923.

25. Ibid., August 18, 1923.

26. Coolidge, *The Autobiography of Calvin Coolidge,* 196.

27. Ibid., 197.

28. Edmund W. Starling and Thomas Sugrue, *Starling of the White House,* 209.
29. Press conference of April 16, 1917, in Howard H. Quint and Robert H. Ferrell, eds., *The Talkative President: The Off-the-Record Press Conferences of Calvin Coolidge,* 73.
30. Dennis, *Gods and Little Fishes,* 25.
31. Coolidge, *Autobiography,* 197.
32. Irwin H. Hoover, *Forty-Two Years in the White House,* 127.
33. Sullivan diary, September 18, November 29, 1923.
34. Press conference of April 22, 1927, in Quint and Ferrell, eds., *Talkative President,* 30.
35. Hibben to Coolidge, January 15, 1924, reel 9; Irvine to Coolidge, November 18, 1923, alumni association to Coolidge, August 31, 1928, reel 2, Coolidge private papers, Forbes Library.
36. Fuess, *Calvin Coolidge,* 327.
37. "Coolidge, Calvin," box 457, Bernays papers, Library of Congress. The occasion was October 17.
38. This is the theme of Donald R. McCoy, *Calvin Coolidge: The Quiet President,* 155, 294.
39. Ibid., 103.

Five. The United States in World Affairs: 1919–1945

Originally published in John A. Garraty, ed., *Interpreting American History: Conversations with Historians,* 2:195–222.
1. I changed this appraisal in *The Strange Deaths of President Harding.*
2. The years since this interview have seen the publication of, among others, *Franklin and Winston: An Intimate Portrait of an Epic Friendship,* by Jon Meacham, and *Roosevelt and Churchill: Men of Secrets,* by David Stafford.

Six. Harry S. Truman: A Chance President in the New World of Superpowers

Originally published in *Prologue: Quarterly of the National Archives* 26 (fall 1994): 153–65.
1. In the poll of historians conducted in 1980 by Steve Neal for the *Chicago Tribune,* Truman ranked eighth.
2. For material that follows see my *The Dying President: Franklin D. Roosevelt, 1944–1945* and *Choosing Truman: The Democratic Convention of 1944.*
3. Robert H. Ferrell, ed., *FDR's Quiet Confidant: The Autobiography of Frank C. Walker,* 134–49.
4. For the election of 1940 see my *Truman and Pendergast,* 80–128.
5. McCullough, *Truman,* 311–12; Edward J. Flynn, *You're the Boss.*
6. Joseph M. Jones, *The Fifteen Weeks (February 21–June 5, 1947).*

7. Dexter Perkins, *The American Approach to Foreign Policy.*

8. In discussions within the cabinet of President James Monroe, Secretary of State John Quincy Adams argued in favor of a Monroe Doctrine because the nations of Europe otherwise would think the United States was supporting British naval supremacy.

9. Michael J. Hogan, *The Marshall Plan: America, Britain, and the Reconstruction of Western Europe, 1947–1952.*

10. Edward J. Drea, *MacArthur's Ultra: Codebreaking and the War against Japan, 1942–1945.*

11. David A. Rosenberg, "U.S. Nuclear Stockpile 1945 to 1950." The possibility of the radar-fusing mechanism's having been compromised is in Samuel R. Williamson Jr. and Steven L. Rearden, *The Origins of U.S. Nuclear Strategy,* 125. The bombing of Dayton is in Harry R. Borowski, *A Hollow Threat: Strategic Air Power and Containment before Korea,* 167.

Sources

Archives and Libraries

Bodleian Library, Oxford University
    James Bryce papers (microfilm)
Calvin Coolidge Memorial Foundation, Plymouth Notch, Vermont
Forbes Library, Northampton, Massachusetts
    Calvin Coolidge, private papers (microfilm)
Franklin D. Roosevelt Library, Hyde Park, New York
Harry S. Truman Library, Independence, Missouri
Herbert Hoover Library, West Branch, Iowa
    William R. Castle Jr. papers
    Mark Sullivan, copy of diary
Houghton Library, Harvard University, Cambridge, Massachusetts
    William R. Castle Jr. diary
Library of Congress, Washington, D.C.
    Newton D. Baker papers
    Edward L. Bernays papers
    Stephen Bonsal papers
    Joel T. Boone papers
    Charles H. Brent papers
    James G. Harbord papers
    Theodore Roosevelt Jr. papers
National Archives, College Park, Maryland
    J. S. Fair papers, box 507, record group 165

Public Record Office, London, England
    Arthur Balfour papers
Jan Shipps, Bloomington, Indiana
    Reed Smoot diary
University of Massachusetts, Amherst
    Dean Albertson papers
University of Toledo, Toledo, Ohio
    Randolph C. Downes papers
University of Wyoming, Laramie
    Francis Russell papers
Western Reserve Historical Society, Cleveland
    Myron T. Herrick papers
Yale University, New Haven, Connecticut
    Edward M. House papers

Oral Histories

Rublee, George. Oral History Collection, Columbia University.
Washburn, Stanley. Oral History Collection, Columbia University.

Books and Articles

Adams, Samuel Hopkins, *Incredible Era: The Life and Times of Warren Gamaliel Harding.* Boston: Houghton Mifflin, 1939.
Allen, Frederick Lewis. *Only Yesterday: An Informal History of the Nineteen-Twenties.* New York: Harper, 1931.
Allen, George E. *Presidents Who Have Known Me.* New York: Simon and Schuster, 1950.
Alperovitz, Gar. *Atomic Diplomacy: Hiroshima and Potsdam.* New York: Simon and Schuster, 1965.
Anthony, Carl S. *Florence Harding: The First Lady, the Jazz Age, and the Death of America's Most Scandalous President.* New York: William Morrow, 1998.
Baruch, Bernard M. *American Industry in the War.* New York: Prentice-Hall, 1941.
Beard, Charles A. *President Roosevelt and the Coming of the War, 1941: A Study in Appearances and Realities.* New Haven: Yale University Press, 1948.

Beaver, Daniel R. *Newton D. Baker and the American War Effort, 1917–1918.* Lincoln: University of Nebraska Press, 1966.

Borowski, Harry R. *A Hollow Threat: Strategic Air Power and Containment before Korea.* Westport, Conn.: Greenwood, 1982.

Britton, Nan. *The President's Daughter.* New York: Elizabeth Ann Guild, 1927.

Burner, David. *Herbert Hoover: A Public Life.* New York: Knopf, 1979.

Burns, James MacGregor. *Roosevelt: The Lion and the Fox.* New York: Harcourt, Brace, 1956.

———. *Roosevelt: Soldier of Freedom.* New York: Harcourt, Brace, 1970.

Chancellor, William Estabrook. *Warren Gamaliel Harding: President of the United States.* Dayton, Ohio: Sentinal Press, 1923.

Chandler, Alfred D., Jr., and Stephen Salsbury. *Pierre S. Du Pont and the Making of the Modern Corporation.* New York: Harper and Row, 1971.

Clarkson, Grosvenor B. *Industrial America in the World War: The Strategy behind the Line, 1917–1918.* Boston: Houghton Mifflin, 1923.

Coffman, Edward M. *The Hilt of the Sword: The Career of Peyton C. March.* Madison: University of Wisconsin Press, 1966.

———. *The War to End All Wars: The American Military Experience in World War I.* New York: Oxford University Press, 1968.

Coolidge, Calvin. *The Autobiography of Calvin Coolidge.* New York: Cosmopolitan, 1929.

Cooper, John Milton, Jr. *The Warrior and the Priest: Woodrow Wilson and Theodore Roosevelt.* Cambridge: Harvard University Press, 1983.

Cramer, C. H. *Newton D. Baker: A Biography.* Cleveland: World, 1961.

Cuff, Robert D. *The War Industries Board: Business Government Relations during World War I.* Baltimore: Johns Hopkins University Press, 1973.

Dallek, Robert. *Franklin D. Roosevelt and American Foreign Policy: 1932–1945.* New York: Oxford University Press, 1979.

Davis, Donald E., and Eugene P. Trani. *The First Cold War: The Legacy of Woodrow Wilson in U.S.-Soviet Relations.* Columbia: University of Missouri Press, 2002.

Dawson, Joseph G. III, ed. *Commanders in Chief: Presidential Leadership in Modern Wars.* Lawrence: University Press of Kansas, 1993.

Debo, Angie. *A History of the Indians of the United States.* Norman: University of Oklahoma Press, 1970.

Dennis, Alfred P. *Gods and Little Fishes.* Indianapolis: Bobbs-Merrill, 1931.

DeWeerd, Harvey A. *President Wilson Fights His War: World War I and the American Intervention*. New York: Macmillan, 1968.

Donovan, Robert J. *Conflict and Crisis: The Presidency of Harry S. Truman, 1945–1948*. 1977. Reprint. Columbia: University of Missouri Press, 1996.

————. *Tumultuous Years: The Presidency of Harry S. Truman, 1949–1953*. 1982. Reprint. Columbia: University of Missouri Press, 1996.

Downes, Randolph C. "The Harding Muckfest." Courtesy of Kenneth W. Duckett, Eugene, Oregon.

————. *The Rise of Warren Gamaliel Harding, 1865–1920*. Columbus: Ohio State University Press, 1970.

Drea, Edward J. *MacArthur's Ultra: Codebreaking and the War against Japan, 1942–1945*. Lawrence: University Press of Kansas, 1991.

Duckett, Kenneth W. "The Harding Papers: How Some Were Burned . . ." *American Heritage* 6 (February 1965): 29–30.

Dunar, Andrew J. *The Truman Scandals and the Politics of Morality*. Columbia: University of Missouri Press, 1984.

Fausold, Martin L. *The Presidency of Herbert C. Hoover*. Lawrence: University Press of Kansas, 1985.

Ferrell, Robert H. *American Diplomacy in the Great Depression: Hoover-Stimson Foreign Policy, 1929–1933*. New Haven: Yale University Press, 1957.

————. *Choosing Truman: The Democratic Convention of 1944*. Columbia: University of Missouri Press, 1994.

————. *The Dying President: Franklin D. Roosevelt, 1944–1945*. Columbia: University of Missouri Press, 1998.

————. *Frank B. Kellogg, Henry L. Stimson*. New York: Cooper Square, 1963.

George C. Marshall. New York: Cooper Square, 1966.

————. *Harry S. Truman*. Washington, D.C.: Congressional Quarterly Press, 2003.

————. *Harry S. Truman: A Life*. Columbia: University of Missouri Press, 1994.

————. *Harry S. Truman and the Modern American Presidency*. Boston: Little, Brown, 1983.

————. *Peace in Their Time: The Origins of the Kellogg-Briand Pact*. New Haven: Yale University Press, 1952.

———. *The Presidency of Calvin Coolidge.* Lawrence: University Press of Kansas, 1998.

———. *The Strange Deaths of President Harding.* Columbia: University of Missouri Press, 1996.

———. *Truman: A Centenary Remembrance.* New York: Viking, 1984.

———. *Truman and Pendergast.* Columbia: University of Missouri Press, 1999.

———. *Woodrow Wilson and World War I, 1917–1921.* New York: Harper and Row, 1985.

Ferrell, Robert H., ed. *The Autobiography of Harry S. Truman.* 1980. Reprint. Columbia: University of Missouri Press, 2002.

———. *Dear Bess: The Letters from Harry to Bess Truman, 1910–1959.* 1983. Reprint. Columbia: University of Missouri Press, 1998.

———. *FDR's Quiet Confidant: The Autobiography of Frank C. Walker.* Niwot: University Press of Colorado, 1997.

———. *Off the Record: The Private Papers of Harry S. Truman.* 1980. Reprint. Columbia: University of Missouri Press, 1997.

Fite, Gilbert C. *Peter Norbeck: Prairie Statesman.* Columbia: University of Missouri, 1948.

Flynn, Edward J. *You're the Boss.* New York: Viking, 1947.

Freidel, Frank. *Franklin D. Roosevelt: A Rendezvous with Destiny.* Boston: Little, Brown, 1990.

Fuess, Claude M. *Calvin Coolidge: The Man from Vermont.* Boston: Houghton Mifflin, 1940.

Garraty, John A., ed. *Interpreting American History: Conversations with Historians.* New York: Macmillan, 1970.

Gilbert, Clinton W. *Behind the Mirrors: The Psychology of Disintegration at Washington.* New York: Putnam's, 1922.

———. *The Mirrors of Washington.* New York: Putnam's, 1921.

Graff, Henry F., ed. *The Presidency: A Reference History.* 2nd ed. New York: Scribner's, 1996.

Hamby, Alonzo L. *Beyond the New Deal: Harry S. Truman and American Liberalism.* New York: Columbia University Press, 1973.

———. *Man of the People: A Life of Harry S. Truman.* New York: Oxford University Press, 1995.

Haynes, John Earl, ed. *Calvin Coolidge and the Coolidge Era: Essays on the History of the 1920s.* Washington, D.C.: Library of Congress, 1998.

Heckscher, August. *Woodrow Wilson: A Biography.* New York: Scribner's, 1991.

Heller, Francis H. "Harry S. Truman: The Writing of His Memoirs." In George Egerton, ed., *Political Memoir: Essays on the Politics of Memory.* London: Cass, 1994.

Heller, Francis, and Robert H. Ferrell. "Plain Faking." *American Heritage* 46 (May–June 1995): 14–16.

Heller, Milton F., Jr. *The Presidents' Doctor: An Insider's View of Three First Families.* New York: Vantage, 2000.

Hewes, James E. *From Root to McNamara: Army Organization and Administration, 1900–1963.* Washington, D.C.: Government Printing Office, 1975.

Hogan, Michael J. *The Marshall Plan: America, Britain, and the Reconstruction of Western Europe, 1947–1952.* New York: Cambridge University Press, 1987.

Hoover, Herbert. *Memoirs.* 3 vols. New York: Macmillan, 1951–1952.

Hoover, Irwin H. *Forty-two Years in the White House.* Boston: Houghton Mifflin, 1934.

Ickes, Harold L. *The Secret Diary of Harold L. Ickes: The Lowering Clouds, 1939–1941.* New York: Simon and Schuster, 1954.

Jenkins, Roy. *Truman.* New York: Harper and Row, 1986.

Jones, Howard. *"A New Kind of War": America's Global Strategy and the Truman Doctrine in Greece.* New York: Oxford University Press, 1989.

Jones, Joseph M. *The Fifteen Weeks (February 21–June 5, 1947).* New York: Viking, 1955.

Kennan, George F. *American Diplomacy: 1900–1950.* Chicago: University of Chicago Press, 1951.

Kimmel, Husband E. *Admiral Kimmel's Story.* Chicago: Regnery, 1955.

Kirkendall, Richard S., ed. *Harry's Farewell: Interpreting and Teaching the Truman Presidency.* Columbia: University of Missouri Press, 2004.

———. *The Harry S. Truman Encyclopedia.* Boston: G. K. Hall, 1989.

Knock, Thomas J. *To End All Wars: Woodrow Wilson and the Quest for a New World Order.* New York: Oxford University Press, 1992.

Lane, Anne W., and Louise H. Wall, eds. *The Letters of Franklin K. Lane: Personal and Political.* Boston: Houghton Mifflin, 1922.

Lee, R. Alton. *Harry S. Truman: Where Did the Buck Stop?* New York: Lang, 1991.

Leuchtenburg, William E. *Franklin D. Roosevelt and the New Deal.* New York: Harper, 1963.

Link, Arthur S. *Wilson: The Road to the White House.* Princeton: Princeton University Press, 1947.

———. *Woodrow Wilson: A Brief Biography.* Cleveland: World, 1963.

Link, Arthur S., et al., eds. *The Papers of Woodrow Wilson.* 69 vols. Princeton: Princeton University Press, 1966–1994.

Longworth, Alice Roosevelt. *Crowded Hours: Reminiscences of Alice Roosevelt Longworth.* New York: Scribner, 1933.

Lukacs, John. *Churchill: Visionary. Statesman. Historian.* New Haven: Yale University Press, 2002.

———. *The End of the Twentieth Century and the End of the Modern Age.* New York: Ticknor and Fields, 1993.

———. *A New History of the Cold War.* Garden City, N.Y.: Doubleday, 1966.

———. *A New Republic: A History of the United States in the Twentieth Century.* New Haven: Yale University Press, 2004.

———. *Year Zero.* Garden City, N.Y.: Doubleday, 1978.

McCoy, Donald R. *Calvin Coolidge: The Quiet President.* New York: Macmillan, 1967.

———. *The Presidency of Harry S. Truman.* Lawrence: University Press of Kansas, 1984.

McCullough, David, *Truman.* New York: Simon and Schuster, 1992.

McFarland, Keith D., and David L. Roll. *Louis Johnson and the Arming of America: The Roosevelt and Truman Years.* Bloomington: Indiana University Press, 2005.

May, Ernest R., ed. *The Ultimate Decision: The President as Commander in Chief.* New York: George Braziller, 1960.

Meacham, Jon. *Franklin and Winston: An Intimate Portrait of an Epic Friendship.* New York: Random House, 2002.

Means, Gaston B. *The Strange Death of President Harding: From the Diaries of Gaston B. Means, a Department of Justice Investigator.* New York: Guild, 1930.

Miller, Merle. *Plain Speaking: An Oral Biography of Harry S. Truman.* New York: Putnam's, 1974.

Miller, Richard Lawrence. *Truman: The Rise to Power.* New York: McGraw-Hill, 1986.

Moos, Malcolm, ed. *A Carnival of Buncombe.* Baltimore: Johns Hopkins University Press, 1956.

Morison, Elting E. "Newton D. Baker." In *Dictionary of American Biography, Supplement Two,* 17–19. New York: Scribner's, 1958.

Murray, Robert K. *The Harding Era: Warren G. Harding and His Administration.* Minneapolis: University of Minnesota Press, 1969.

Murray, Robert K., and Tim H. Blessing. *Greatness in the White House: Rating the Presidents, Washington through Carter.* University Park: Pennsylvania State University Press, 1988.

Neal, Steve. "Putting Presidents in Their Place." *Chicago Sun-Times,* November 19, 1995.

Nevins, Allan. "Warren G. Harding." In *Dictionary of American Biography,* 8:252–57. New York: Scribner's, 1932.

Offner, Arnold A. *American Appeasement: United States Foreign Policy and Germany, 1933–1938.* Cambridge: Belknap Press of Harvard University Press, 1969.

———. *Another Such Victory: President Truman and the Cold War, 1945– 1953.* Stanford: Stanford University Press, 2002.

———. *The Origins of the Second World War: American Foreign Policy and World Politics, 1917–1941.* New York: Praeger, 1975.

Osgood, Robert E. *Ideals and Self-Interest in America's Foreign Relations: The Great Transformation of the Twentieth Century.* Chicago. University of Chicago Press, 1953.

Palmer, Frederick. *Newton D. Baker: America at War.* 2 vols. New York: Dodd, Mead, 1931.

Pemberton, William E. *Harry S. Truman: Fair Dealer and Cold Warrior.* Boston: Twayne, 1989.

Pepper, George Wharton. *Philadelphia Lawyer: An Autobiography.* Philadelphia: Lippincott, 1944.

Perkins, Dexter. *The American Approach to Foreign Policy.* Cambridge: Harvard University Press, 1952.

Phillips, Cabell. *The Truman Presidency: The History of a Triumphant Succession.* New York: Macmillan, 1966.

Poen, Monte M., ed. *Strictly Personal and Confidential: The Letters Harry Truman Never Mailed.* 1982. Reprint. Columbia: University of Missouri Press, 1999.

Potter, David M. "Sketches for the Roosevelt Portrait." *Yale Review* 39 (September 1949): 39–53.

Quint, Howard H., and Robert H. Ferrell, eds. *The Talkative President: The Off-the-Record Press Conferences of Calvin Coolidge.* Amherst: University of Massachusetts Press, 1964.

Ridings, William, Jr., and Stuart B. McIver. "1990s Presidential Poll." *Presidential Studies Quarterly* 25 (1994–1995): 375–77.

Rosenberg, David A. "U.S. Nuclear Stockpile 1945 to 1950." *Bulletin of the Atomic Scientists* 35 (May 1982): 26.

Russell, Francis. "The Four Mysteries of Warren Harding." *American Heritage* 14 (April 1963): 9–10, 81–86.

———. *The Shadow of Blooming Grove: Warren G. Harding and His Times.* New York: McGraw-Hill, 1968.

Schermerhorn, Jane. "The Love Affair That Never Died: Exclusive Interview with Nan Britton," *Detroit News,* February 24, 1965.

Schlesinger, Arthur M., Jr. *The Age of Roosevelt.* 3 vols. Boston: Houghton Mifflin, 1957–1960.

Seymour, Charles. "End of a Friendship?" *American Heritage* 14 (August 1963): 4–6.

Sinclair, Andrew. *The Available Man: The Life behind the Masks of Warren Gamaliel Harding.* New York: Macmillan, 1965.

———. "The Dear Departed." *New York Times Book Review,* January 22, 1967, 2, 28.

Smith, Richard Norton. *An Uncommon Man: The Triumph of Herbert Hoover.* New York: Simon and Schuster, 1984.

Starling, Edmund W., and Thomas Sugrue. *Starling of the White House.* New York: Simon and Schuster, 1946.

Stueck, William Whitney. *The Road to Confrontation: American Policy toward China and Korea, 1947–1950.* Chapel Hill: University of North Carolina Press, 1981.

———. *Rethinking the Korean War: A New Diplomatic and Strategic History.* Princeton: Princeton University Press, 2002.

Sullivan, Mark. *Our Times: The Twenties.* New York: Scribner's, 1935.

Tansill, Charles C. *Back Door to War: The Roosevelt Foreign Policy, 1933–1941.* Chicago: Regnery, 1952.

Trani, Eugene P., and David L. Wilson. *The Presidency of Warren G. Harding.* Lawrence: Regents Press of Kansas, 1977.

Trask, David F. *The AEF and Coalition Warmaking, 1917–1918.* Lawrence: University Press of Kansas, 1993.

———. *Captains and Cabinets: Anglo-American Naval Relations, 1917–1918.* Columbia: University of Missouri Press, 1972.

———. *General Tasker Howard Bliss and the "Sessions of the World," 1919.* Philadelphia: American Philosophical Society, 1966.

———. *The United States in the Supreme War Council: American War Aims and Inter-Allied Strategy, 1917–1918.* Middletown, Conn.: Wesleyan University Press, 1961.

———. "Woodrow Wilson and the Reconciliation of Force and Diplomacy, 1917–1918." *Naval War College Review* 27 (January–February 1975): 23–31.

Truman, Harry S. *Memoirs.* 2 vols. Garden City, N.Y.: Doubleday, 1955–1956.

Truman, Margaret. *Bess W. Truman.* New York: Macmillan, 1986.

———. *Harry S. Truman.* New York: Morrow, 1973.

Unterberger, Betty Miller. *The United States, Revolutionary Russia, and the Rise of Czechoslovakia.* Chapel Hill: University of North Carolina Press, 1989.

White, William Allen. *Autobiography.* New York: Macmillan, 1946.

———. *Calvin Coolidge: The Man Who Is President.* New York: Macmillan, 1925.

———. *Masks in a Pageant.* New York: Macmillan, 1928.

Whiteman, Harold B., ed. *Charles Seymour: Letters from the Paris Peace Conference.* New Haven: Yale University Press, 1965.

Williamson, Samuel R., Jr., and Steven L. Rearden. *The Origins of U.S. Nuclear Strategy.* New York: St. Martin's, 1993.

Wilson, Joan Hoff. *Herbert Hoover: Forgotten Progressive.* Boston: Little, Brown, 1975.

Index